FREEDOM

ALSO BY OSHO

FREEDOM

The Courage to
Be Yourself

OSHO

·

Insights for a
New Way of Living

St. Martin's Griffin ✠ New York

10   9   8   7   6   5

Freedom means the capability to say <u>yes when yes is needed</u>, to say <u>no when no is needed</u>, and sometimes to keep quiet when <u>nothing is needed</u>—to be silent, not to say anything. When all these dimensions are available, there is freedom.

—*Osho*

Contents

Contents

Foreword

THREE DIMENSIONS OF FREEDOM

Freedom is a three-dimensional phenomenon. The first is the physical dimension. You can be enslaved physically, and for thousands of years man has been sold in the marketplace just like any other commodity. Slaves have existed all over the world. They were not given human rights; they were not really accepted as human beings, they were thought of as subhuman. And people are still being treated as subhuman. In India there are *sudras*, the untouchables. Much of India is still living in slavery; there are still parts of the country where these people cannot be educated, cannot move into other professions than those decided by tradition five thousand years ago. Even to touch them is thought to make you impure; you have to take a bath immediately. Even if you don't touch the person, but only his shadow—then too you have to take a bath.

And all over the world, the woman's body is not considered equal to the man's body. She is not as free as man is. In China for centuries the husband had the right to kill his wife without being punished because the wife was his possession. Just as you can destroy your chair or you can burn your house—because it is your chair, it is your house—it was your wife. In Chinese law there was no punishment for the husband if he killed his wife, because she was thought to be soulless. She was just a reproductive mechanism, a factory to produce children.

So there is physical slavery and there is physical freedom—that your body is not enchained, that it is not categorized as lower than anybody else's, that there is an equality as far as the body is concerned. But even today this freedom does not exist everywhere. It is becoming less and less so but it has not disappeared completely.

Freedom of the body will mean that there is no distinction between black and white, that there is no distinction between man and woman, that there is no distinction of any kind as far as bodies are concerned. Nobody is pure, nobody is impure; all bodies are the same.

This is the very basis of freedom.

Then there is the second dimension: psychological freedom. There are very few individuals in the world who are psychologically free . . . because if you are a Mohammedan you are not psychologically free; if you are a Hindu you are not psychologically free. Our whole way of bringing up children is to make them slaves—slaves of political ideologies, social ideologies, religious ideologies. We don't give them a chance to think on their own, to search on their own. We force their minds into a certain mold. We stuff their minds with things—things that even we are not experienced in. Parents teach children that there is a God—and they know nothing of God. They tell their children that there is heaven and there is hell—and they know nothing of heaven and hell.

> ❧
>
> Our whole way of bringing up children is to make them slaves— slaves of political ideologies, social ideologies, religious ideologies. We don't give them a chance to think on their own, to search on their own.

You are teaching your children things that you don't know yourself. You are just conditioning their minds because your minds were conditioned by your parents. This way the disease goes on from one generation to another generation.

Psychological freedom will be possible when children are allowed to grow, helped to grow to more intellect, more intelligence, more consciousness, more alertness. No belief will be given to them. They will not be taught any kind of faith, but they will be given as much incentive as possible to search for truth. And they will be reminded from the very beginning: "Your own truth, your own finding, is going to liberate you; nothing else can do that for you."

Truth cannot be borrowed. It cannot be studied in books. Nobody can inform you about it. You have to sharpen your intelligence yourself, so that you can look into existence and find it. If a child is left open, receptive, alert, and given the incentive for search, he will have psychological freedom. And with psychological freedom comes tremendous responsibility. You don't have to teach it to him; it comes like the shadow of psychological freedom. And he will be grateful to you. Otherwise every child is angry at his parents because they have ruined him: they destroyed his freedom, they conditioned his mind. Even before he asked any questions, they filled his mind with answers that are all bogus—because they are not based on his own experience.

The whole world lives in psychological slavery.

> Truth cannot be borrowed. It cannot be studied in books. Nobody can inform you about it. You have to sharpen your intelligence yourself, so that you can look into existence and find it.

And the third dimension is the ultimate of freedom—which is knowing that you are not the body, knowing that you are not the mind, knowing that you are only pure consciousness. That knowledge comes through meditation. It separates you from the body, it separates you from the mind, and ultimately only you are there as pure consciousness, as pure awareness. That is spiritual freedom.

These are the three basic dimensions of freedom for the individual.

The collective has no soul, the collective has no mind. The collective has no body even; it is only a name. It is just a word. For the collective, there is no need for freedom. When all the individuals are free, the collective will be free. But we are very impressed by words, so much so that we forget that words don't have any substance. The collective, the society, the community, the religion, the church—they are all words. There is nothing real behind them.

I am reminded of a small story. In *Alice In Wonderland*, Alice is coming to the palace of the queen. When she arrives the queen asks her, "Did you meet a messenger on the way coming towards me?"

And the little girl says, "Nobody. I met nobody."

And the queen thought "nobody" was somebody, so she asks, "But then why has Nobody not reached here yet?"

The little girl said, "Madam, nobody is nobody!"

And the queen said, "Don't be stupid! I understand: Nobody must be Nobody, but he should have arrived before you. It seems Nobody walks slower than you do."

And Alice said, "That is absolutely wrong! Nobody walks faster than me!"

In this way the dialogue continues. Through the whole dialogue, "nobody" becomes somebody, and it is impossible for Alice to convince the queen that "nobody" is nobody.

The collective, the society—all these are just words. That which really exists is the individual; otherwise there will be a problem. What is the freedom of a Rotary Club? What is the freedom of the Lions Club? These are just names.

The collective is a very dangerous idea. In the name of the collective the individual, the real, has always been sacrificed. I am absolutely against it.

Nations have been sacrificing individuals in the name of the nation—and "nation" is just a word. The lines that you have drawn on the map are not anywhere on the earth. They are just your game. But fighting over those lines that you have drawn on the map, millions of people have died—real people dying for unreal lines. And you make them heroes, national heroes!

This idea of the collective has to be destroyed completely; otherwise in some way or other we will continue sacrificing the individual. We have sacrificed the individual even in the name of religion, in religious wars. A Mohammedan dying in a religious war knows that his paradise is certain. He has been told by the cleric, "If you are dying for Islam then your paradise is absolutely certain, with all the pleasures you have ever imagined or dreamt of. And the person you have killed will also reach paradise because he has been killed by a Mohammedan. It is a privilege for him, so you need not feel guilty that you have killed a man." Christians have crusades—a jihad, a religious war—and kill thousands of people, burn living human beings. For what? For some collectivity—for Christianity, for Buddhism, for Hinduism, for communism, for fascism, anything will do. Any word representing some collectivity, and the individual can be sacrificed.

There is no reason for the collectivity even to exist: individuals are enough. And if individuals have freedom, are psychologically free, are spiritually free, then naturally the collective will be spiritually free.

The collective consists of individuals, not vice versa. It has been said that the individual is only a part of the collective; that is not true. The individual is not just a part of the collective; the collective is only a symbolic word for individuals meeting together. They are not parts of anything; they remain independent. They remain organically independent, they don't become parts of a collective.

If we really want a world of freedom, then we have to understand that in the name of the collectivity so many massacres have happened that now it is time to stop. All collective names should lose the grandeur that they have had in the past. Individuals should be the highest value.

The freedom *from* something is not true freedom. The freedom to do anything you want to do is also not the freedom I am talking about. My vision of freedom is to be yourself.

> ➳
>
> Freedom *from* something is not true freedom. The freedom to do anything you want to do is also not the freedom I am talking about. My vision of freedom is to be yourself.

It is not a question of getting freedom *from* something. That freedom will not be freedom, because it is still given to you; there is a cause to it. The thing that you were feeling dependent on is still there in your freedom. You are obliged to it. Without it you would not have been free.

The freedom to do anything you want is not freedom either, because wanting, desiring to "do" something, arises out of the mind— and mind is your bondage.

The true freedom comes out of choiceless awareness, but when there is choiceless awareness the freedom is neither dependent on things nor dependent on doing something. The freedom that follows choiceless awareness is the freedom just to be yourself. And you are yourself already, you are born with it; hence it is not dependent on anything else. Nobody can give it to you and nobody can take it from you. A sword can cut your head but it cannot cut your freedom, your being.

It is another way of saying that you are centered, rooted in your natural, existential self. It has nothing to do with outside.

Freedom from things is dependent on the outside. Freedom to do something is also dependent on the outside. Freedom to be ultimately pure has not to be dependent on anything outside you.

You are born as freedom. It is just that you have been conditioned to forget it. Layers upon layers of conditionings have made you a puppet. The strings are in somebody else's hands. If you are a Christian, you are a puppet. Your strings are in the hand of a God that does not exist, so just to give you the sense that God exists there are prophets, messiahs, representing God.

They represent nobody, they are just egoistic people—and even the ego wants to reduce you to a puppet. They tell you what to do, they give you Ten Commandments. They give you your personality—that you are a Christian, a Jew, a Hindu, a Mohammedan. They give you your so-called knowledge. And naturally, under the great burden that they start giving you from the very beginning of your childhood—the Himalayan load you are carrying—underneath it, hidden, repressed, is your natural self. If you can get rid of all conditionings, if you can think that you are neither a communist nor a fascist, that you are neither a Christian nor a Mohammedan . . .

You were not born a Christian or Mohammedan; you were born just pure, innocent consciousness. To be again in that purity, in that innocence, in that consciousness, is what I mean by freedom.

> You are born as freedom. It is just that you have been conditioned to forget it.

Freedom is the ultimate experience of life. There is nothing higher than that. And out of freedom many flowers blossom in you.

Love is the flowering of your freedom. Compassion, another flowering of your freedom.

All that is valuable in life flowers in the innocent, natural state of your being.

So don't connect freedom with independence. Independence is naturally *from* something, *from* somebody. Don't connect freedom with doing things that you want to do, because that is your mind, not you. Wanting to do something, desiring to do something, you are in the bondage of your wanting and your desiring. With the freedom I am talking about, you simply *are*—in utter silence, serenity, beauty, bliss.

FREEDOM

UNDERSTANDING THE ROOTS OF SLAVERY

To be totally free one needs to be totally aware, because our bondage is rooted in our unconsciousness; it does not come from the outside. Nobody can make you unfree. You can be destroyed but your freedom cannot be taken away unless you give it away. In the ultimate analysis it is always your desire to be unfree that makes you unfree. It is your desire to be dependent, your desire to drop the responsibility of being yourself, that makes you unfree.

The moment one takes responsibility for oneself . . . And remember it is not all roses, there are thorns in it; it is not all sweet, there are many bitter moments in it. The sweet is always balanced by the bitter, they always come in the same proportion. The roses are balanced by the thorns, the days by the nights, the summers by the winters. Life keeps a balance between the polar opposites. So one who is ready to accept the responsibility of being oneself with all its beauties, bitternesses, its joys and agonies, can be free. Only such a person can be free. . . .

Live it in all its agony and all its ecstasy—both are yours. And always remember: ecstasy cannot live without agony, life cannot exist without death, and joy cannot exist without sadness. That's how things are—nothing can be done about it. That's the very nature, the very Tao of things.

Accept the responsibility of being yourself as you are, with all that is good and with all that is bad, with all that is beautiful and that which is not beautiful. In that acceptance a transcendence happens and one becomes free.

SOCIETY AND FREEDOM OF THE INDIVIDUAL–AN INTERVIEW

Social rules seem to be a basic need for human beings. Yet no society has ever helped man to realize himself. Can you please explain what kind of relationship exists between individuals and society, and how they can help each other to evolve?

> If man really becomes human—not only in name but in reality—he will not need any rules. Very few people have realized that up to now.

It is a very complex question, but very fundamental too. In the whole of existence, only man needs rules. No other animal needs any rules.

The first thing that has to be understood is that there is something artificial about rules. The reason man needs them is that he has left being an animal, yet he has not become human; he is in a limbo. That is the need for all the rules. If he were an animal there would be no need. Animals live perfectly well without any rules, constitutions, laws, courts. If man really becomes human—not only in name but in reality—he will not need any rules.

Very few people have realized that up to now. For example, for men like Socrates, Zarathustra, Bodhidharma, there is no need of any rules. They are alert enough not to do any harm to anybody. There is no need for any laws, for any constitutions. If the whole society evolves to be authentically human, there will be love but there will not be law.

The problem is that man needed rules, laws, governments, courts, armies, a police force, because he lost the natural behavior of an animal and he has not yet gained a new natural status again. He is just in between. He is nowhere, he is a chaos. To control that chaos all these things are needed.

The problem becomes more complex, because the forces that have been evolved to control man—religions, states, courts—have grown so powerful. They had to be given power; otherwise, how would they control people? So we fell into a kind of slavery on our own. Now that these institutions have become powerful, they don't want to drop their vested interests. They don't want man to evolve.

You are asking how man and the society, the individual and the society can evolve. You do not understand the problem at all. If the individual evolves, the society dissolves. The society exists only because the individual is not allowed to evolve. All these powers have for centuries been controlling man, and enjoying their power and their prestige. They are not ready to let man evolve, to let man grow to a point where they and their institutions will become useless. There are many situations that will help you to understand.

It happened in China, twenty-five centuries ago:

Lao Tzu became very famous, a wise man, and he was without doubt one of the wisest men ever. The emperor of China asked him very humbly to become his chief of the supreme court, because nobody could guide the country's laws better than he could. He tried to persuade the emperor, "I am not the right man," but the emperor was insistent.

Lao Tzu said, "If you don't listen to me . . . just one day in the court and you will be convinced that I am not the right man, because the *system* is wrong. Out of humbleness I was not saying the truth to you. Either I can exist or your law and your order and your society can exist. So . . . let us try it."

> If there are going to be too many poor people and only a few rich people, you cannot stop thieves, you cannot stop stealing. The only way to stop it is to have a society where everybody has enough to fulfill his needs, and nobody has unnecessary accumulation just out of greed.

The first day a thief who had stolen almost half the treasures of the richest man in the capital was brought into the court. Lao Tzu listened to the case and then he said that the thief and the richest man should both go to jail for six months.

The rich man said, "What are you saying? I have been stolen from, I have been robbed—what kind of justice is this, that you are sending me to jail for the same amount of time as the thief?"

Lao Tzu said, "I am certainly being unfair to the thief. Your need to be in jail is greater, because you have collected so much money to yourself, deprived so many people of money . . . thousands of people are downtrodden and you are collecting and collecting money. For what? Your very greed is creating these thieves. You are responsible. The first crime is yours."

Lao Tzu's logic is absolutely clear. If there are going

to be too many poor people and only a few rich people, you cannot stop thieves, you cannot stop stealing. The only way to stop it is to have a society where everybody has enough to fulfill his needs, and nobody has unnecessary accumulation just out of greed.

The rich man said, "Before you send me to jail I want to see the emperor, because this is not according to the constitution; this is not according to the law of the country."

Lao Tzu said, "That is the fault of the constitution and the fault of the law of the country. I am not responsible for it. Go and see the emperor."

The rich man said to the emperor, "Listen, this man should be immediately deposed from his post; he is dangerous. Today I am going into jail, tomorrow you will be in jail. If you want to save yourself, this man has to be thrown out; he is absolutely dangerous. And he is very rational. What he is saying is right; I can understand it—but he will destroy us!"

The emperor understood it perfectly well. "If this rich man is a criminal, then I am the greatest criminal in the country. Lao Tzu will not hesitate to send me to jail."

Lao Tzu was relieved of his post. He said, "I tried to tell you before; you are unnecessarily wasting my time. I told you I am not the right man. The reality is that your society, your law, and your constitution are not right. You need wrong people to run this whole wrong system."

The problem is that the forces we created to keep man from falling apart into chaos are now so powerful that they don't want to leave you free to grow—because if you are capable of growing, becoming an individual, alert, aware and conscious, there will be no need of all these people. They will all lose their jobs, and with their jobs they will lose their prestige, their power, their leadership, their priesthood, their popehood—everything will be gone. So now those who were needed in the beginning for protection have turned into the enemies of humanity.

My approach is not to fight against these people, because they are powerful, they have armies, they have money, they have everything. You cannot fight with them, you will be destroyed. The only way out of this mess is to silently start growing your own consciousness, which they cannot prevent by any force. In fact, they cannot even know what is going on inside you.

I offer you the alchemy of inner transformation. Change your inner being. And the moment you are changed, completely transformed, you will suddenly see you are out of the imprisonment, you are no longer a slave. You were a slave because of your chaos.

It happened in the Russian revolution:

The day the revolution succeeded, one woman started walking in Moscow in the middle of the road. The policeman said, "This is not right. You cannot walk in the middle of the road."

The woman said, "Now we are free."

> Change your inner being. And the moment you are changed, completely transformed, you will suddenly see you are out of the imprisonment, you are no longer a slave. You were a slave because of your chaos.

Even if you are free, you will have to follow the rules of traffic; otherwise traffic will become impossible. If cars and people are running everywhere they want, turning wherever they want, don't take any note of the lights, people will be simply getting into accidents, and being killed. This will bring the army in, to enforce the law that you have to walk—to the right or to the left, whichever is chosen by the country, but nobody can walk in the middle. Then, at the point of a gun, you will have to follow the rules. I always remember that woman; she is very symbolic.

Freedom does not mean chaos. Freedom means more responsibility, so much responsibility that nobody need interfere in your life. That you can be left alone, that the government need not interfere with you, that the police need not interfere with you, that the law has nothing to do with you—you are simply outside of their world.

This is my approach—if you really want to transform humanity, each individual should start growing on his own. And, in fact, a crowd is not needed for growth.

Growth is something like a child growing in a mother's womb. No crowd is needed; the mother has just to be careful. A new man has to be born in you. You have to become the womb of a new human being. Nobody will come to know about it, and it is better that nobody knows about it. You simply go on doing your ordinary work, living in the ordinary world, being simple and ordinary—not becoming a revolutionary, reactionary, punk or skinhead. That is not going to help. That is sheer stupidity. I understand that it is because of frustration, but still it is insane. The society is insane and out of frustration you become insane? The society is not afraid of such people; the society is afraid only of people who can become so centered, so conscious that laws become useless for them. They always do right. They are beyond the grip of the so-called powerful interests.

If individuals grow, society will diminish. The way they have known society—with the government, with the army, with the courts, with the policemen, with the jails—this society will diminish. Certainly, because there are so many human beings, new forms of collectivities will come into being. I would not like to call them "society," just to avoid the confusion between the words. I call the new collectivity a commune. The word is significant: it means a place where people are not only living together but where people are in deep communion.

To live together is one thing; we are doing it: in every city, every town, thousands of people are living together—but what togetherness is there? People don't even know their neighbors. They live in the same skyscraper, thousands of people, and they never come to know that they are living in the same house. It is not togetherness because there is no communion. It is simply a crowd, not a community. So I would like to replace the word *society* with the word *commune*.

Society has existed on certain basic principles. You will have to remove them, otherwise the society will not disappear. The first and the most important unit of society has been the family: if the family remains the way it is, then the society cannot disappear, the church cannot disappear; then religions cannot disappear. Then we cannot create one world, one humanity.

The family is psychologically out of date. It is not that it was always there; there was a time when there was no family, people lived in tribes. The family came into existence because of private property. There were powerful people who managed to have more private property than anybody else, and they wanted it to be given to their children. Up to that time there was no question of family. Men and women were meeting out of love; there was no marriage and no family. But once property came into existence, the man became very possessive of the woman. He turned the woman also into part of his property.

In Indian languages the woman is actually called "property." In China the woman was so much a property that even if a husband killed his wife there was no law against it. No crime was committed—you were absolutely free to destroy your own property. You can burn your furniture, you can burn your house—it is not a crime, it is your house. You can kill your wife. . . .

With private property the woman also became private property, and every strategy was used so that the man could be absolutely certain that the child that was born from his wife was really his.

Now, this is a difficult problem: the father can never be absolutely certain; only the mother knows. But the father created every kind of barrier against the movement of the woman so that she could not come into contact with other men. All possibilities and all doors were closed.

It is not a coincidence that only old women go into your churches and temples, because for centuries that was the only place they were allowed to go, knowing perfectly well that the church is protective of the family. The church knows that once the family is gone, the church is gone. And the church of course is the last place where some romantic affair might happen. They have taken every precaution. And the priest has to be celibate—these are guarantees—the priest is celibate, he is against sex, he is against women, in different religions in different ways.

The Jaina monk cannot touch a woman; in fact, the woman should not come closer than eight feet to the Jaina monk. The Buddhist monk is not allowed to touch a woman. There are religions that don't allow women to enter their religious places, or they have partitions to separate them. Men occupy the main part of the temple or the mosque, the women have a small area but it is separate. The men cannot even see them; meeting someone is impossible.

Many religions, like Islam, have covered their women's faces. Mohammedan women's faces have become pale because they never see the sunlight. Their faces are covered, their bodies are covered in every possible way. The woman is not to be educated because education gives people strange kinds of thoughts. People start thinking, people start arguing. . . .

The woman was not allowed to have a paid career because that meant independence. She was cut off at every corner just for a simple reason, so that the man could be certain that his son was really his son. Those who were really powerful—for example, kings—had male servants castrated, because they were moving in the palace, working and serving others. They had to be castrated; otherwise, there was a danger. . . . And there was danger because every emperor had hundreds of wives, many of whom he would never see. Naturally they could fall in love with anybody. But only castrated men were allowed into the palace, so even if the women fell in love they could not create children. That was the important thing.

The family has to disappear and give place to the commune. A commune means that we have pooled all our energies, all our money, everything into a single pool—and this will take care of all the people. The children will belong to the commune, so there is no question of individual heritage. And if you pool all your energies, all your money, and all your resources, every commune can be rich and every commune can enjoy being alive equally.

Once individuals are growing and communes are growing side by side, society will disappear, and with society all the evils that the society has created.

I will give you one example.

In China a revolutionary step was taken two thousand years ago. Under the new system the doctor had to be paid by the patient as long as the patient remained healthy. If the patient fell sick, then the doctor was not to be paid. That seems very strange. We pay the doctor when we are sick, and he makes us healthy again. But this is dangerous, because you are making the doctor dependent on your sickness. Sickness becomes his interest: the more people fall sick, the more he can earn. His interest becomes not health but sickness.

If everybody remains healthy, then the doctor will be the only one who will be sick!

They came up with a revolutionary idea, very practical, that every person would have his or her own physician, and as long as the person remains healthy the doctor is paid every month. It is the duty of the doctor to keep the person healthy—and naturally he will do that, because he is being paid for it. If the patient falls sick, the doctor loses money. When there are epidemics, the doctor goes bankrupt.

Right now it is just the opposite. I have heard this story:

The doctor came to Mullah Nasruddin and said, "You have not paid and I have been again and again coming and reminding you that I cured your child of smallpox, and you don't listen."

Mullah said, "You had better listen; otherwise I am going to sue you in the court."

The doctor said, "This is strange. . . . I treated your child."

Mullah said, "Yes, that I know—but who spread the epidemic to the whole town? My child! So all the money that you have earned, you have to divide with me."

He was right. His child had done a great job, and since that day the doctor never came back again to ask for the money. Mullah's analysis was right. The doctor had earned plenty out of the epidemic.

But this is a very wrong system. The commune should pay the doctor to keep the commune healthy, and if anybody gets sick in the commune the doctor's salary should be cut. So health is the business of the doctor, not sickness. And you can see the difference: in the West the doctor's business is called "medicine," which relates to sickness. In the East it is called "*ayurveda*," which means "the science of life"—not of sickness. The basic business of the doctor should be that people live long, live healthy, whole, and he should be paid for it. So each commune easily could afford to keep a doctor, a plumber, an engineer—whatever services are needed. That should be the commune's responsibility, and the people who serve the commune should be rotated so no power center rises again.

The members of the managing committee of the commune should change every year; new people should be coming in and old people going out, so nobody becomes addicted to power. Power is the worst drug that people can become addicted to; it should be given, but in very small doses and not for a long time. Let the individual grow and let the commune grow.

> Forget all about society, don't fight with it. Have nothing to do with society, let society go on as it is. If it wants to live it will have to change its form, its structure. If it wants to die, let it die.

But for now, forget all about society; don't fight with it. Have nothing to do with society; let society go on as it is. If it wants to live, it will have to change its form, its structure. If it wants to die, let it die. There is no harm. The world is overpopulated; it needs only one-fourth of its population. So the old rotten heads who cannot conceive of anything new, who are absolutely blind and cannot see that what they are doing is harmful and poisonous . . . if they have decided to die, then let them die silently. Don't disturb them.

I don't teach you to be revolutionaries. I want you to be very silent, almost underground transformers. Because all the revolutions have failed, now the only possible way is that we should do it so silently and peacefully that it can happen.

There are things which happen only in silence. For example, if you love trees, you should not take up the sapling every day to look at its roots; otherwise you will kill it. Those roots have to remain hidden. Silently they go on doing their work.

My people have to be just like roots: silently go on doing the work, changing themselves, changing anybody who is interested; spreading the methods that can change; creating small pools, small groups, small communes, and wherever possible bigger communes. But let this whole thing happen very silently, without creating any upheaval.

The individual can exist only if society dies; the two cannot coexist. It is time for the society to be dead, and we will find new ways of togetherness which will not be formal, which will be more of the heart. The family prevents it. The family draws a boundary around every child. It says, "I am your father, so love me. I am your mother, so love me. This is your family. If there is a need, sacrifice yourself for the family." The same idea is projected on a bigger scale as the nation: "This is your nation. If it needs you, sacrifice yourself." Family, society, nation . . . it is the same idea becoming bigger and bigger.

> The family is the root cause of all our problems. Our poverty, our sickness, our madness, our emptiness, our lovelessness—the family is the cause.

So my basic critique is of the family. The family is the root cause of all our problems. Our poverty, our sickness, our madness, our emptiness, our lovelessness—the family is the cause. And the family is the cause of all our conditionings. From the very beginning it starts conditioning your mind: "You are a Jew, you are a

Christian, you are a Hindu, you are this and you are that"—and the poor child does not know what nonsense you are talking about.

I have heard about a rabbi and a bishop:

They lived opposite each other, and naturally they were continually competing with each other about everything. It was a question of the prestige of their respective religions.

One morning the rabbi saw the bishop had gotten a new car. He asked, "What are you doing?"

The bishop was pouring water over the car. He said, "I am baptizing it. I got a new car—a Cadillac."

The rabbi was heartbroken. Seeing with his own eyes, outside his own front door the car was being made Christian!

Next day when the bishop came out, he was surprised. He asked the rabbi, "What are you doing?"

A beautiful Rolls Royce was standing there and the rabbi was cutting the exhaust pipe. He said, "I am circumcising my Rolls Royce. Now it is a Jew!"

This is what they are doing with every child. And every child is as innocent as the Cadillac and the Rolls Royce; he does not know what is being done to him.

The family is the ground of all conditionings; it gives you as inheritance the whole past and the load, the burden of all those things that have been proved wrong for hundreds of years. You are loaded with all those wrong things, and your mind is closed and clogged and it cannot receive anything new that goes against it. Your mind is simply full of wrong things.

If the children are in the hands of the commune—I have experimented and found it immensely successful. The children are happier because they are freer. No conditioning is stamped on them; they mature earlier, and because nobody is trying to make them dependent they become independent. Nobody is going out of their way to help them, so they have to learn how to help themselves. This brings maturity, clarity, a certain strength. And they are all meditating: meditation is not a conditioning; it is simply sitting silently, doing nothing, just enjoying the silence—the silence of the night, the silence of the early morning . . . and slowly, slowly you become acquainted with the silence that pervades your inner being. Then the moment you close your eyes you fall into the pool of a silent lake, which is fathomless. And out of that silence you are rejuvenated every moment.

Out of that silence comes your love, your beauty, a special depth to your eyes; a special aura to your being, a strength to your individuality, and a self-respect.

Individual freedom and authority on one side, and authoritarianism and dictatorship on the other side, move man's life and his aspirations. Please comment on this.

It is the same problem, the same question, phrased differently. Society is authoritarian; the church is authoritarian; the educational system is authoritarian. They all say, "Whatever we say is right and you need not question it. You have simply to follow."

And there are problems, for example in the educational system. I have been a student, I have been a professor, and I know that for the best part of life a person is being ruined by authoritarian people in the schools, in the colleges, in the universities.

I was expelled from many colleges for the simple reason that I could not accept any authoritarianism. I said, "You prove it and I am ready to accept it. But without proving it, without giving the right arguments for it, without making it a rational statement, I am not going to accept it." And I was fighting in every subject class, because in every class the teachers were simply lecturing. Students were taking notes, because all that was needed was to repeat in the examination papers what the teachers had been telling them. And the better you repeat, exactly like a parrot, the more credit you get.

But those professors had difficulty even proving small things, and it became embarrassing to them. Every day it became an issue. Anything they said, I would stand up immediately and inquire— and I was asking relevant questions—"On what grounds . . . ?"

For example, one of the professors who was teaching religions made the statement that the *Vedas*—the Hindu holy scriptures— were written by God. I had to protest. I said, "I object. In the first place you have not been able to prove the existence of God. In the second place, now you are saying that these books, which are full of rubbish, were written by God. Have you ever looked into the *Vedas*?" I asked him, "Have you ever read from the first page to the last page?" There are four *Vedas*, big volumes. "I have brought all the four with me, and at random I can open and read, and let the whole class decide whether this is a statement which God could have written."

The *Vedas* are full of prayers. Now, *God* cannot pray; to whom will he be praying? And prayers for such stupid things that it is simply ridiculous to say that they are written by God. One Brahmin is praying, "I have been continuously doing all the rituals, living according to the scriptures and you have still not given me a child. Give me a child; that will be a proof that my prayers have been heard."

I asked him, "How could God have written this passage? It is written by someone and addressed to God, but it cannot be written by God himself. And if this is the situation of God, then that poor fellow should not be bothered about it. God is asking about a child from somebody else, so why should we not ask from the same source? Why should we bother this poor fellow?"

Finally every college would reject me. That was their answer.

The principal would tell me, "We are sorry. We know you are right, but we have to run the college. You will destroy the whole institution. Professors are threatening to resign, students are saying that you don't allow the professors to teach, because on a single point every day the whole period is lost. Eight months have passed and the course will not be finished in the coming two months if the same pattern continues.

"They have come here to pass examinations; they are not in-terested in truth, they are not interested in the validity of any state-ment. Their only reason to be here is to get a certificate. And you are a strange fellow—you don't seem to be interested in certifi-cates."

I said, "I am not interested at all in certificates. What will I do with the certificates from these professors who don't know any-thing? I cannot think of these people as my examiners. The day you give me the certificate, I will tear it up immediately in front of you—because these people can't answer the simplest questions."

But the whole system is geared in that way. When I became a professor myself, I had to make a new arrangement. The arrange-ment was that in each forty-minute period, for twenty minutes I would teach the syllabus as it was written in the books, and for twenty minutes I would criticize it. My students said, "We will go mad!"

I said, "That is *your* problem—but I cannot leave these state-ments to stand without criticism. You can choose; when your ex-amination comes you can choose to write whichever you want. If you want to fail, choose my part. If you want to pass, choose the first part. I am making it clear; I am not deceiving anybody—but I cannot go on deceiving you by teaching you something I think is absolutely wrong."

The vice-chancellor finally had to call me in, and he said to me, "This is a strange type of teaching. I have been receiving re-ports every day that half the time you teach the syllabus and half the time you have your arguments, which destroy the whole lesson that you have taught them. So they come out of the classroom as empty as they had gone in . . . in fact in more of a mess!"

I said, "I'm not worried about anybody. What have they done with me all these years when I was a student? I was expelled from one college and then another. And you can come one day and listen as to whether I am doing any injustice to the prescribed course. When I teach the prescribed course, I do it as totally as possible, to make it clear."

He came one day and he listened, and after twenty minutes he said, "That is really great. I also had been a student of philosophy, but nobody has ever taught me about it this way."

I said, "This is only half the lesson. You just wait, because now I am going to destroy it completely, step by step."

And when I destroyed it completely, he said, "My God! Now I can understand what the poor students are reporting to me. You are not supposed to be a professor in this kind of institution. I can understand that what you are doing is absolutely honest, but this system does not create people of intelligence; this system only creates people of good memory—and that's what is needed. We need clerks, we need bureaucrats—and those jobs don't need intelligence, they need a good memory."

I said, "In other words you need computers, not human beings. If this is your educational system, then sooner or later you are going to replace human beings with computers"—and that's what they are doing. Everywhere they are replacing important positions with computers, because computers are more reliable. They are just memory, no intelligence.

A human being has a certain intelligence, however repressed.

The man who dropped atom bombs on Hiroshima and Nagasaki—if it had been a computer, there would be no question: at the exact time, at the exact mileage, it would have dropped the bomb and returned. It would have been simply mechanical. But the man who was dropping the bomb, however you may have destroyed his intelligence, had to think twice about what he was doing. Killing one hundred thousand people who were absolutely innocent, who were civilians, who were not in the military, who had not done any harm to anybody—is it right?

Now everywhere, all nuclear weapons are in the hands of computers, not in the hands of humans. Computers will fight the third world war. Humans will be killed—that is another matter. Computers don't care whether humanity survives or disappears; it does not matter to them. But they will do exact and efficient work, which a man cannot do. A man may hesitate in destroying the whole of humanity. Something of intelligence, just a little bit of intelligence is enough to create the question, "What am I doing?"

All our institutions, our religions, are authoritarian. They don't tell you why: "Just do it because it is written in the book, because Jesus says so." Jesus has not given a single argument for why it should be done; he has not given a single rational ground for any of his doctrines. Neither has Moses done that, nor has Krishna.

> Computers will fight the third world war. Humans will be killed—that is another matter. Computers don't care whether humanity survives or disappears; it does not matter to them. But they will do exact and efficient work, which a man cannot do.

Krishna simply says to Arjuna, "This is from God: You have to fight." This is authoritarianism. And God is used, manipulated in every situation to make whatever you are saying absolutely unquestionable.

We have to destroy all authoritarianism in the world.

Authority is totally different. Authoritarianism is connected with the society, with the church; authority is something which is concerned with the individual realization.

If I say something to you, I say it with authority. This simply means I am saying it because this is my *experience*—but it does not mean that you have to believe it. It is enough that you listened to it; now you can think it over, you can decide for or against it.

To me what is important is not that you decide *for* it; what is important to me is that you decide *on your own*. Your decision may be against it, it does not matter—but the decision should come from your own being. If it doesn't come from your own being, then *you* are making me authoritarian.

I am speaking from my authority. Please don't make me into an authoritarian, because I am simply stating the fact with as much force and fire as I am capable of—so that it is absolutely clear to you, and now you are free to decide. I am not deciding for you, and I am not asking you to have faith in me or believe in me.

I am simply asking, "Give me a little chance. Think about what I am saying to you"—and I will be grateful that you thought about it. That's enough. Your thinking will give you a sharper intelligence . . . and I trust in intelligence. If you think, and your intelligence becomes sharper, I know whatever you conclude will be right.

And even if you conclude wrong one time, it does not matter. One has to fall many times and rise up again. That's how life is. One has to make mistakes and learn from them, and change every blocking rock into a stepping-stone.

But around me there is no question of any belief or faith. With individual freedom, authoritarianism dies and a new force arises: authority. Each individual is capable of having experiences of his own; then he has authority, then he can say, "I have seen it. I have tasted it. I have enjoyed it. I have danced it. And it is not a question that I am quoting from some scripture, I am simply opening my heart to you."

Authority belongs to experience.

Authoritarianism belongs to somebody else, not to you; hence it creates slavery, not freedom. And to me freedom is the ultimate value, because only in freedom can you blossom, and can you blossom to your fullest possibility.

Is society a real fact determined by the existence of man, or is it a false concept, a conditioning which exists only because man is asleep?

Society is not an existential reality. It is created by man because man is asleep, because man is in chaos, because man is not capable of having freedom without turning it into licentiousness. Man is not capable of having freedom and not taking advantage of it. So it is an artificial—but necessary—creation of man.

Because society is artificial, it can be dissolved. Because it was necessary once, it does not mean it has to be necessary forever. Man just has to change those conditions which made it necessary. And it is good that it is not existential, otherwise there would be no way to get rid of it.

It is our own manufactured thing. We can destroy it any day we want.

How to evolve out of the collectivity, the nations, without falling into the barbarity of single egos fighting against each other?

All your questions are centered on one thing. I would like to give you one answer.

I am reminded of a parable:

A great master was sitting on the seashore, on the beach, and a man who was seeking for truth came to him, touched his feet and asked, "If I am not disturbing you, I would like to do anything that you suggest which can help me to find the truth."

The master simply closed his eyes and remained silent. The man shook his head. He said in his own mind, "This man seems to be crazy. I am asking him a question and he is closing his eyes." He shook the man and said, "What about my question?"

The master said, "I answered it. Just sit silently . . . don't do anything, and the grass grows by itself. You need not bother about it—everything will happen. You just sit silently, enjoy silence."

The man said, "Can you give it a name—because people will be asking me, 'What are you doing?'"

So he wrote on the sand with his finger: meditation.

The man said, "This is too short an answer. Be a little more elaborate."

The master wrote in big letters: MEDITATION.

The man said, "But these are simply big letters. You are writing the same thing."

The old master said, "If I say more than that, then it

> Each individual has to become a meditator, a silent watcher, so that he can discover himself. And this discovery is going to change everything around him. And if we can change many people through meditation, we can create a new world.

will be wrong. If you can understand, then just do what I have told you, and you will know."

And that's my answer too.

Each individual has to become a meditator, a silent watcher, so that he can discover himself. And this discovery is going to change everything around him. And if we can change many people through meditation, we can create a new world.

Many people have been hoping for centuries for a new world, but they had no idea how to create it. I am giving you the exact science for how to create it. Meditation is the name of that science.

THE PROBLEM OF GOD

There is a prophetic saying of Nietzsche's: "God is dead and man is free." He had tremendous insight into the matter. Very few people have been able to understand the depth of his statement. It is a milestone in the history of consciousness.

If there is a God, man can never be free—that is an impossibility. God and man's freedom cannot coexist, because the very meaning of God is that he is the creator; then we are reduced to puppets. And if he can create us, he can destroy us at any moment. He never asked us when he created us—he is not obliged to ask us when he wants to destroy us. It is purely his whim to create or to destroy. How can you be free? You are not free even to be. Even your birth is not your freedom, nor is your death your freedom—and between these two slaveries do you think your life can be freedom?

God has to die if man's freedom is to be saved.

The choice is clear; there is no question of any compromise. With God man will remain a slave and freedom will remain just an empty word. Only without God does freedom start having meaning.

But Friedrich Nietzsche's statement is only half; nobody has tried to make it complete. It looks complete, but appearances are not always true. Friedrich Nietzsche was not aware that there are religions in the world which have no God—yet even in those religions man is not free. He was not aware of Buddhism, Jainism, Taoism—the most profound religions of all. For all these three religions there is no God.

For the same reason Lao Tzu, Mahavira, and Gautam Buddha have denied God—because they could see that with God, man is just a puppet. Then all efforts for enlightenment are meaningless; you are not free, how can you become enlightened? And there is somebody omnipotent, all-powerful—he can take away your enlightenment. He can destroy anything!

> Just by making God dead you cannot make man free. You will have to make one more thing dead—and that is religion.

But Nietzsche was not aware that there have been religions that are godless. For thousands of years there have been people who have understood that God's existence is the greatest barrier to man's freedom—they removed God. But still man is not free.

What I am trying to lead you to understand is that just by making God dead you cannot make man free. You will have to make one more thing dead—and that is religion.

That's why I said religion also has to die; it has to follow God. And we have to create a religiousness which is godless and religionless, which has nobody "above" more powerful than you, and no organized religion to create different kinds of cages—Christian, Muslim, Hindu, Buddhist. Beautiful cages . . .

With God and religion both dead, one more thing dies automatically and that is the priesthood, the leader, the different forms

24

of religious leader. Now he has no function. There is no organized religion in which he can be a pope or a shankaracharya or an ayatollah. He has no God whom he can represent; his function is finished.

Buddha, Mahavira, Lao Tzu dropped God in the same way as Friedrich Nietzsche—not knowing, not aware that if religion remained even without God, the priest would manage to keep man in slavery. And he *has* kept man in slavery.

So to complete the insight of Friedrich Nietzsche, religion has to die. There is no point of an organized religion if there is no God. For whom does the organized religion exist? The churches, the temples, the mosques, the synagogues have to disappear. And with that the rabbis and the bishops and all kinds of religious leaders become simply jobless, they become useless. But a tremendous revolution happens: man becomes utterly free.

Before I can talk about the implications of this freedom you have to understand: if Friedrich Nietzsche's insight is complete, then what kind of freedom will be available to human beings? God is dead, man is free . . . free for what? His freedom will be just like any other animal's.

It is not right to call it freedom—it is licentiousness. It is not freedom because it does not carry any responsibility, any consciousness. It will not help man to raise himself upwards, to become something higher than he is in his slavery. Unless freedom takes you higher than what you were in your slavery, it is meaningless. It is possible your freedom may take you lower than your slavery, because the slavery had a certain discipline, it had a certain morality, it had certain principles. It had a certain organized religion to look after you, to keep you afraid of punishment and hell, to keep you greedy for rewards and heaven, and to keep you a little above the wild animal, who has freedom, but that freedom has not made him a higher being. It has not given him any quality that you can appreciate.

Nietzsche had no idea that just to give freedom is not enough; it is not only not enough, it is dangerous. It may reduce man to animality. In the name of freedom he may lose his path toward higher states of consciousness.

When I say that God is dead, religion as an organized body is dead—then man is free to be himself. For the first time he is free to explore his innermost being with no hindrances. He is free to dive into the depths of his being, rise to the heights of his consciousness. There is nobody to hinder him; his freedom is total. But this freedom is possible only if—with God going out of existence, religion going out of existence, priesthood and religious leadership going out of existence—we can save something that I call the quality of religiousness, so that only religiousness is alive. And religiousness is perfectly harmonious with human freedom; it enhances human growth.

By "religiousness" I mean that man, as he is, is not enough. He can be more, he can be so much more. Whatever he is, is only a seed. He does not know what potential he is carrying within himself.

> *Man, as he is, is not enough. He can be more, he can be so much more. Whatever he is, is only a seed. He does not know what potential he is carrying within himself.*

Religiousness simply means a challenge to grow, a challenge for the seed to come to its ultimate peak of expression, to burst forth in thousands of flowers and release the fragrance that was hidden in it. That fragrance I call religiousness. It has nothing to do with your so-called religions, it has nothing to do with God, it has nothing to do with priesthood; it has something to do with you and your possibilities of growth.

THE IDEA OF FATE AND DESTINY

There is no fate, no destiny. You are just trying to dump your responsibility on something that does not exist. And because it does not exist, it cannot resist you; it cannot say, "Please don't dump your responsibility on me!"

God is silent, you can dump anything on him—no resistance, because there is nobody to resist. Fate is again the same. You fail in love, you fail in other matters. It hurts that you have failed. You need some kind of ointment for your wounded heart. "Fate" is a beautiful ointment, and freely available. You don't have to pay for it. You can say, "What can I do?—everything is decided by fate." Success or failure, richness or poverty, sickness or health, life or death—everything is in the hands of an unknown power called fate. "I am doing my best, still I go on failing. I am following all the moral principles preached to me, still I am poor. And I see all kinds of immoral people becoming richer, getting ahead, becoming famous. It is all fate." It gives you solace. It gives you solace that you are not reaching your goals.

> You fail in love, you fail in other matters. It hurts that you have failed. You need some kind of ointment for your wounded heart. "Fate" is a beautiful ointment, and freely available.

It also gives you solace that if others have achieved success, there is nothing much in it; it is just decided by fate. So, on the one hand, you are saved from feeling inferior; on the other hand, your jealousy enjoys the idea that the successful person is successful only

27

because fate has determined it that way: "It has nothing to do with him; he's not superior to me."

God, fate, destiny—they are all in the same category: throwing your responsibility onto something that does not exist.

If God existed he would not remain silent. I am continually saying he does not exist. If he existed, it is time—he should have appeared and announced, "I am here! Why do you go on saying that I don't exist?" But he will never come.

There have always been people who have denied the existence of God, but he has never made any effort to prove himself. For example, Edmund Burke, one of the famous philosophers of the West, stood in a church and said to the priest, "This is my watch. If God exists—I don't want big proof, just a simple proof—my watch should stop moving. You pray, your congregation can pray, you do anything that you want to do. Persuade your God to stop my watch, and that will be enough to convert me."

> God, fate, destiny—
> they are all in the
> same category:
> throwing your
> responsibility onto
> something that does
> not exist.

They prayed—it was a question of the prestige of the whole of Christianity, a single man challenging God. And he was not asking for a big miracle, just a small miracle: "Stop my watch moving." And God could not do that. Edmund Burke has proved that there is no God. What an argument!—but it is simple, clear, relevant.

All over the world, you go on dumping anything that you want to get rid of on God, on fate, on destiny. They are just different names for nonexistential things. Certainly you cannot throw your garbage on somebody who is actually there. There is a limit to patience. You just try throwing your garbage onto the property of your neighbor. Perhaps for one day he may not say anything; perhaps for two days he may wait—but how long? Sooner or later he is going to grab you by the neck and prove to you: "I exist! You cannot go on throwing your garbage in my yard." But if there is nobody in the house, you can continue to throw the garbage in the yard as long as you want. Nobody will resist, nobody will come out and say, "What is going on? Don't you have any sense of decency in you?"

God, fate, destiny—these are bogus words, mumbo jumbo, nothing more than that. Drop them completely, because dropping them will make you an individual, fully responsible for your acts. And unless you take the responsibility on yourself, you will never become strong, you will never become independent, you will never taste freedom.

You can have freedom. But the cost is to accept responsibility in its totality.

I have felt such immense freedom that looking at you I feel sad. You have the same opportunity, the same potential to blossom into a free individual, but you go on remaining a slave. And the way you manage it is by never being responsible.

> You can have freedom. But the cost is to accept responsibility in its totality.

You think not being responsible makes you free? Not feeling responsible for your actions, for your thoughts, for your being, do you think you are freed from all the consequences? No, absolutely not. It makes you a slave; it makes you something subhuman. It takes all glory away from you. You cannot stand straight; you become a hunchback. Your intelligence cannot grow because you have not accepted the challenge. You are waiting for fate, for destiny, for God. You are thinking, "When the time comes—the right time, God willing—I will be blissful too."

There is no God who can decide your blissfulness. You are alone in existence. You come alone, you die alone. Between birth and death, of course you can deceive yourself that someone is with you—your wife, your father, your mother, your husband, your friend—but this is just make-believe. You come alone, you go alone; you are alone between birth and death.

And I am not saying that you cannot love a man or a woman. In fact, when two independent, free people, who take responsibility on their own shoulders, meet, there is immense beauty in it. Nobody is a burden to the other. Nobody is dumping anything onto the other. You have dropped the very idea of dumping anything. You can be together but your aloneness remains untouched, pure, crystal-clear, virgin. You never trespass on each other's territories. You can enjoy each other just because you are separate.

The more separate you are—the more clearly it is understood that you are alone, she is alone—the more there is a possibility of a great meeting of two alonenesses, two purities, two individuals.

Forget words like destiny, fate, kismet, God. And don't allow yourself to be cheated by astrologers, mind readers, palmists, predictors of your future. There is no future if you don't create it! And whatsoever is going to be tomorrow

> When two independent, free people, who take responsibility on their own shoulders, meet, there is immense beauty in it. Nobody is a burden to the other. Nobody is dumping anything onto the other. You have dropped the very idea of dumping anything.

is going to be your creation. And it has to be done today, now—because out of today, today's womb, tomorrow will be born.

Take the responsibility totally on yourselves—that's my message to you. That's why I am always trying to destroy the God in your mind. I have nothing against him. How can I have anything against him?—he does not exist! Do you think I am wasting my time fighting with something that does not exist? No, I am fighting with your conditionings—they exist. God does not exist, but an idea of God exists in you and I am fighting with that idea, telling you to drop it, be clean, and take the whole responsibility for your life.

This is my experience: the day I took complete responsibility for myself, I found the doors of freedom opening to me. They go together.

Everybody wants freedom. Nobody wants responsibility. You will never have freedom; you will remain a slave. Remember, remaining a slave is also your responsibility. You have chosen it; it has not been forced upon you.

I am reminded of Diogenes, a beautiful Greek philosopher, mystic—and a mystic of a rare quality. He was a contemporary of Aristotle, and he was as much against Aristotle as I am, so I have a certain friendship with Diogenes.

Aristotle defined man as an animal without feathers who walks on two legs. What did Diogenes do? He caught an animal—and there are many animals who walk on two legs, but they have feathers also, they can fly. Diogenes caught a peacock, he took out all the feathers—and he sent the peacock to Aristotle with the message: "Please receive the gift of a human being."

Diogenes used to live naked because, he said, "Man is born naked, and he becomes weaker because he is protected by clothes." All around the world no animal has clothes—except a few dogs in England. England is a mysterious country. Dogs have clothes because a naked dog is un-Christian. You will be surprised to learn that in Victorian England even chair legs were covered with clothes, because they are legs and it is not gentlemanly to look at naked legs.

Diogenes lived naked. He was a strong man. Four people who were hijacking people and selling them as slaves in the market thought, "This is a great catch, this man can bring us a lot of money. We have sold many slaves, but none of them were so strong, so beautiful, so young. We can get as high a price as we demand; and there is going to be a great competition in the marketplace when we put this man on the pedestal for sale. But," they thought, "four are not enough to catch him. He alone could kill us all."

Diogenes heard what they were saying about him. He was sitting by the side of the river, just enjoying the cool breeze of the evening, underneath a tree; and behind the tree those four were planning what to do. He said, "Don't be worried. Come here! You need not worry that I will kill you, I never kill anything. And you need not worry that I will fight, resist you—no. I don't fight anybody, I don't resist anything. You want to sell me as a slave?"

Embarrassed, afraid, those four people said, "That's what we were thinking. We are poor . . . if you are willing?"

He said, "Of course I am. If I can help you in your poverty in some way, it is beautiful."

So they brought out chains. He said, "Throw them in the river; you need not chain me. I will walk ahead of you. I don't believe in escaping from anything. In fact, I am getting excited about the idea of being sold, standing on a high pedestal, and hundreds of people trying to get me. I am excited about this auction—I am coming!"

Those four people became a little more afraid: this man is not only strong and beautiful, he seems to be mad also; he could be dangerous. But now there was no way for them to escape. He said, "If you try to escape, you will be risking your own life. Just follow me, all four of you. Put me on the pedestal in the market."

Unwillingly they followed him. They wanted to take him, but he went ahead of them! You see the point? Even in such a situation, he was taking the responsibility on himself. He was a free man even in such a situation, where people were conspiring and trying to sell him in the marketplace, which is the ugliest thing that can happen to a man—to be sold like a commodity, auctioned off.

But he told those people, "Don't be afraid, and don't try to escape. You have given me a great idea, I am grateful to you. This is my responsibility, I am going to the marketplace. You put me up for auction."

What type of man was this? they wondered. But there was no way to back out now, so they followed him. And when he was put on a high pedestal so that everybody could see, there was almost silence, pin-drop silence. People had never seen such a proportionate body, so beautiful—as if made of steel, so strong.

Before the auctioneer said anything, Diogenes declared, "Listen, people! Here is a master to be sold to any slave, because these four poor people need money. So start the auction; but remember, you are purchasing a master."

A king purchased him. Of course, he could do it—more and more money he offered at the auction. Many people were interested but finally a sum, larger than any that had ever been heard of before, was given to those four people. Diogenes said to them, "Are you happy now? You can leave now, and I will go with this slave."

On the way to the palace as they were riding in the chariot, the king said to Diogenes, "Are you crazy or something? You think yourself a master? I am a king, and you think me a slave?"

Diogenes said, "Yes, and I am not crazy, but you are crazy. I can prove it right now." At the back of the chariot was the queen. Diogenes said, "Your queen is already interested in me, she is finished with you. It is dangerous to purchase a master."

The king was shocked. Of course, he was nothing in comparison to Diogenes. He took out his sword and asked his queen,

"What he is saying, is it true? If you say the truth, your life will be saved—that is my promise. But if you say an untruth, and I find it out later on, I will behead you."

Fearful, afraid, still the queen said, "It is true. Before him, you are nothing. I am enchanted, allured; the man has some magic. You are just a poor guy compared to him. This is the truth."

Of course, the king stopped the chariot and told Diogenes, "Get out of the chariot. I set you free; I don't want to take such risks in my palace."

> Take responsibility! And then even in utter poverty, suffering, imprisoned in a jail, you will remain completely a master of yourself.

Diogenes said, "Thank you. I am a man who cannot be made a slave, for the simple reason that every responsibility I take on myself. I have not left those four people feeling guilty—they did not bring me there, I came of my own accord. They must be feeling obliged. And it is your chariot, if you want me to get out, that is perfectly good. I am not accustomed to chariots at all, my legs are strong enough. I am a naked man, a golden chariot does not fit with me."

Take responsibility! And then even in utter poverty, suffering, imprisoned in a jail, you will remain completely a master of yourself. You will have the freedom that comes with responsibility.

All your religions have been making you dependent on God, on fate, on destiny. Those are just different names for something nonexistential. What is true is your slavery or your freedom. Choose. If you choose freedom, then you have to destroy all the strategies of others that make you a slave. That's what I am trying to do here: trying to cut all your chains, making you free from everything so that you can be yourself.

And the moment you are yourself, you start growing, you become greener. Flowers start opening up, and there is great fragrance around you.

FEAR OF FLYING

Rabindranath Tagore says in his Gitanjali:

"Obstinate are the trammels, but my heart aches when I try to break them. Freedom is all I want, but to hope for it I feel ashamed. I am certain that priceless wealth is in thee, and that thou art my best friend. But I have not the heart to sweep away the tinsel that fills my room. The shroud that covers me is a shroud of dust and death. I hate it, yet hug it in love. My debts are large, my failures great, my shame secret and heavy. Yet when I come to ask for my good, I quake in fear lest my prayer be granted."

Rabindranath Tagore is the most contemporary man and yet the most ancient, too. His words are a bridge between the modern mind and the world's most ancient sages. In particular, his book *Gitanjali* is his greatest contribution to human evolution, to human consciousness. It is one of the rarest books that has appeared in the twentieth century.

Rabindranath is not a religious person in the ordinary sense. He is one of the most progressive thinkers—untraditional, unorthodox—but his greatness exists in his childlike innocence. And because of that innocence, perhaps he was able to become the vehicle of the universal spirit. He is a poet of the highest category, and also a mystic. Such a combination has happened only once or twice before—in Kahlil Gibran, in Friedrich Nietzsche, and in Rabindranath Tagore. With these three persons, the whole category is complete. In the long history of man, it is extraordinary. There have been great poets and great mystics. There have been great poets with a little mysticism in them, and there have been great mystics who have expressed themselves in poetry—but their poetry is not great.

Rabindranath is in a strange situation.

I have heard about a man who loved two beautiful women and was always in trouble, because even one woman is trouble enough! Both women wanted to know whom he loved the most. They took him for a ride on the lake in a motorboat, and in the middle of the lake they stopped the boat and they told the man: "It has to be decided, because it is heavy on our hearts. . . . Once we know we will become slowly, slowly tolerant about it; we may accept it. But remaining in the dark and always thinking about it has become a wound."

The man said, "What is the matter? Ask directly."

Both the women said together: "Our question is, Whom do you love the most?'"

The man fell into deep silence—it was such a strange situation in the middle of the lake—but he must have been a man of great humor. He said, "I love each of you more than the other." And both women were satisfied. That's what they wanted.

It is difficult to say about Rabindranath whether he is a greater poet or a greater mystic. He is both—greater than each—and in the twentieth century.

Rabindranath was not a man confined to India. He was a world traveler, educated in the West, and he was continually moving around the world to different countries—he loved being a wanderer. He was a citizen of the universe, yet his roots were deep in India. He may have flown far away like an eagle across the sun, but he kept on coming back to his small nest. And he never lost track of the spiritual heritage of India, no matter how covered with dust it may have become. He was capable of cleaning it and making it a mirror in which one can see oneself.

His poems in *Gitanjali* are offerings of songs to existence. That is the meaning of the word *Gitanjali*: offerings of songs. He used to say, "I have nothing else to offer. I am just as poor as a bird, or as rich as a bird. I can sing a song every morning fresh and new, in gratefulness. That is my prayer."

He never went to any temple, he never prayed in the traditional way. He was born a Hindu, but it would not be right to confine him to a certain section of humanity; he was so universal. He was told many times, "Your words are so fragrant with religiousness, so radiant with spirituality, so alive with the unknown that even those who do not believe in anything more than matter become affected, are touched. But you never go to the temple, you never read the scriptures."

His answer is immensely important for you. He said, "I never read the scriptures; in fact I avoid them, because I have my own experience of the transcendent and I don't want others' words to be mixed with my original, authentic, individual experience. I want to offer God exactly what is my heartbeat. Others may have known—certainly, others have known—but their knowledge cannot be my knowledge. Only my experience can satisfy me, can fulfill my search, can give me trust in existence. I don't want to be a believer."

These are the words to be remembered: "I don't want to be a believer; I want to be a knower. I don't want to be knowledgeable; I want to be innocent enough so that existence reveals its mysteries to me. I don't want to be worshiped as a saint." And the fact is, that in the whole of the twentieth century there was nobody else more saintly than Rabindranath Tagore—but he refused to be recognized as a saint.

He said, "I have only one desire—to be remembered as a singer of songs, as a dancer, as a poet who has offered all his potential, all his flowers of being, to the unknown divineness of existence. I don't want to be worshiped; I consider it a humiliation . . . ugly, inhuman, and removed from the world completely. Every man contains God; every cloud, every tree, every ocean is full of godliness, so who is to worship whom?"

Rabindranath never went to any temple, never worshiped any God, was never, in a traditional way, a saint. But to me he is one of the greatest saints the world has known. His saintliness is expressed in each of his words.

Obstinate are the trammels, but my heart aches when I try to break them. Freedom is all I want, but to hope for it I feel ashamed.

He is saying something not only about himself, but about all human consciousness. <u>Such people don't speak about themselves; they speak about the very heart of all mankind.</u>

Obstinate are the trammels. . . . The hindrances are great. The chains that prevent my freedom . . . I have become too attached to them. They are no longer chains to me; they have become my ornaments. They are made of gold, they are very precious. But my heart aches, because on the one hand I want freedom and on the other hand I cannot break the chains that prevent me from being free. Those chains, those attachments, those relationships have become my life. I cannot conceive of myself without my beloved, without my friends. I cannot conceive of myself absolutely alone, in deep silence. My songs have also become my fetters, so *my heart aches when I try to break them. Freedom is all I want.*

This is the situation of every human being. It is difficult to find a man whose heart does not want to fly like a bird in the sky, who would not like to reach to the faraway stars, but who also knows his deep attachment with the earth. His roots are deep in the earth. His split is that he is attached to his imprisonment, and his deepest longing is for freedom. He is divided against himself.

This is the greatest anguish, anxiety. You cannot leave the world that chains you; you cannot leave those who have become your hindrances in life, because they are also your attachments, your joys. They are also in some way a nourishment for your pride. You can neither leave them, nor can you forget that you don't belong to this world, that your home must be somewhere else because in your dreams you are always flying, flying to faraway places.

Freedom is all I want, but to hope for it, I feel ashamed. Why should one feel ashamed to hope for freedom?—because nobody is preventing you. You can be free this very moment. But those attachments . . . they have gone very deep in you; they have become almost your very existence. They may be bringing misery to you but they also bring moments of happiness. They may be creating chains for your feet, but they also give you moments of dance.

It is a very strange situation every intelligent human being has to face: we are rooted in the earth and we want wings to fly in the sky. We cannot be uprooted because the earth is our nourishment, our food. And we cannot stop dreaming of wings, because that is our spirit, that is our very soul, that is what makes us human beings.

No animal feels the anguish; all animals are utterly satisfied as they are. Man is the only animal who is intrinsically discontented; hence, the feeling of shame—because he knows, "I can be free."

I have always loved an ancient story:

> This is the greatest anguish, anxiety. You cannot leave the world that chains you; you cannot leave those who have become your hindrances in life, because they are also your attachments, your joys.

A man, a great man, a fighter for freedom was traveling in the mountains. He stayed in a caravanserai for the night. He was amazed that in the caravanserai there was a beautiful parrot in a golden cage, continually repeating, "Freedom! Freedom!" And it was such a place that when the parrot repeated the word "Freedom!" it would go on echoing in the valleys, in the mountains.

> *No animal feels the anguish, all animals are utterly satisfied as they are. Man is the only animal who is intrinsically discontented, hence, the feeling of shame— because he knows, "I can be free."*

The man thought: I have seen many parrots, and I have thought they must want to be free from those cages . . . but I have never seen such a parrot whose whole day, from the morning to the evening when he goes to sleep, is spent in calling out for freedom. He had an idea. In the middle of the night he got up and opened the door of the cage. The owner was fast asleep and he said to the parrot, he whispered, "Now get out."

But he was very surprised that the parrot was clinging to the bars of the cage. He said to him again and again, "Have you forgotten about freedom? Just get out! The door is open and the owner is fast asleep; nobody will ever know. You just fly into the sky; the whole sky is yours."

But the parrot was clinging so deeply, so hard, that the man said, "What is the matter? Are you mad?" He tried to take the parrot out with his own hands, but the parrot started pecking at him, and at the same time he was shouting, "Freedom! Freedom!" The valleys in the night echoed and re-echoed. But the man was also stubborn, he was a freedom fighter. He pulled the parrot out, and threw him into the sky; and he was very satisfied, although his hand was hurt. The parrot had attacked him as forcefully as he could, but the man was immensely satisfied that he had made a soul free. He went to sleep.

In the morning, as the man was waking up, he heard the parrot shouting, "Freedom! Freedom!" He thought perhaps the parrot must be sitting on a tree, or on a rock. But when he came out, the parrot was sitting in the cage. The door was open.

> The cage has certain securities, safeties. In the cage the parrot has no need to worry about food, has no need to worry about enemies, has no need to worry about a thing in the world. It is cozy, it is golden.

I have loved the story, because it is very true. You may like to be free, but the cage has certain securities, safeties. In the cage the parrot has no need to worry about food, has no need to worry about enemies, has no need to worry about a thing in the world. It is cozy, it is golden. No other parrot has such a valuable cage.

Your power, your riches, your prestige—all are your cages. Your soul wants to be free, but freedom is dangerous. Freedom has no insurance. Freedom has no security, no safety.

Freedom means walking on the edge of a razor—every moment in danger, fighting your way. Every moment is a challenge from the unknown. Sometimes it is too hot, and sometimes it is too cold—and nobody is there to take care of you. In the cage, the owner was responsible. When it was cold, he used to cover the cage with a blanket; he used to put a fan close by when it was too hot.

Freedom means tremendous responsibility; you are on your own and alone.

Rabindranath is right: *Freedom is all I want, but to hope for it, I feel ashamed*—because it is not a question of hope; it is a question of taking a risk.

I am certain that priceless wealth is in thee, and that thou art my best friend. But I have not the heart to sweep away the tinsel that fills my room.

In the world of freedom, in the experience of freedom, you are certain there is priceless wealth. But this certainty is also a projection of your desire, of your longing—how can you be certain? You would *like* to be certain. You know that a longing for freedom is there. It cannot be for a futile freedom; it must be for something rich, something priceless. You are creating a certainty to gather courage so that you can take the jump into the unknown.

. . . *And that thou art my best friend.* But these are all beautiful dreams, these are hopes; the certainty is your own cage, its security. *But I have not the heart to sweep away the tinsel that fills my room.* These are beautiful ideas in the mind.

The shroud that covers me is a shroud of dust and death, I hate it, yet hug it in love.

You know your body is going to die. In fact, your body is made of dead material; it is already dead. It seems alive because something alive is inside it. It radiates warmth and aliveness, because of a guest inside you. The moment that guest has flown away, the reality of the body will be revealed to you.

Rabindranath says our bodies are made of dust and death. *I hate it, and yet hug it in love.* But when you fall in love with a woman, then two skeletons hug each other; both know that the skin is only a covering of a skeleton. If you could see each other in real nudity—not only without clothes, but without the skin, too, because that is the real clothing—then you would be shocked, and you would escape as fast as possible from the beloved with whom you were promising to live forever and forever. You would not even look back; you would not even like to be reminded of the phenomenon.

It happened in the court of one emperor of India, Shahjehan. He was in love with a woman, but the woman was not willing to marry him.

He was a gentleman; otherwise he could have forced her—he tried to persuade her. But she was in love with one of his body-guards. And when he found out about it, he was really enraged. They were both immediately caught and brought to the court.

Shahjehan was going to cut off the heads of both, then and there. But his prime minister, who was a very old man—he had been his father's prime minister and Sahjehan respected him just like a father—said, "Don't do that. Be a little wiser; that is not enough punishment. I will give them the right punishment." He ordered that both should be tied together naked, in a hug, and then chained to a pillar in the court. The other members of the court could not believe it—what kind of punishment is this? This seems to be a reward; that's what they always wanted, to hug each other. But they were wrong.

That old man really had a great psychological insight. Those two lovers also wondered—"What kind of punishment is this? This is a reward!" They hugged each other with great love.

They were tied with a rope, so they could not escape from each other; then they were tied to a pillar. How long can you hug somebody? Five minutes, seven minutes, half an hour . . . ? After twenty-four hours they hated each other . . . they had to, there was no other way. They were perspiring, their body smells filled the place, their excrement . . . and there was no way to escape. After twenty-four hours the old man said, "Now give then their clothes and make them free."

And as they got their clothes, they rushed in opposite directions, never to meet each other again; they had met enough!

The shroud that covers me is a shroud of dust and death. I hate it, yet hug it in love.

Such is the schizophrenia of man, the split personality of man. His house is divided against itself; hence, he cannot find peace.

My debts are large, my failures great, my shame secret and heavy. Yet when I come to ask for my good, I quake in fear lest my prayer be granted.

These lines can be understood only if I remind you of another poem of Rabindranath in the same book, *Gitanjali*.

In that other poem, he says, "I have been seeking and searching God for as long as I can remember, for many, many lives, from the very beginning of existence. Once in a while I have seen him by the side of a faraway star, and I have rejoiced and danced that the distance, although great, is not impossible to reach. And I have traveled and reached to the star; but by the time I reached the star, God has moved to another star. And it has been going on for centuries.

"The challenge is so great that I go on hoping against hope . . . I have to find him, I am so absorbed in the search. The very search is so intriguing, so mysterious, so enchanting that God has become almost an excuse—the search has become itself the goal.

"And to my surprise, one day I reached a house in a faraway star with a small sign in front of it, saying 'This is the house of God.' My joy knew no bounds—so finally I have arrived! I rushed up the steps, many steps, that led to the door of the house. But as I was coming closer and closer to the door, a fear suddenly appeared in my heart. As I was going to knock, I became paralyzed with a fear that I had never known, never thought of, never dreamt of. The fear was: if this house is certainly the house of God, then what will I do after I have found him?

"Now searching for God has become my very life; to have

found him will be equivalent to committing suicide. And what am I going to do with him? I had never thought of all these things before. I should have thought before I started the search: what am I going to do with God?

"I took my shoes in my hands, and silently and very slowly stepped back, afraid that God may hear the noise and may open the door and say, 'Where are you going? I am here, come in!' And as I reached the steps, I ran away as I have never run before; and since then I have been again searching for God, looking for him in every direction—and avoiding the house where he really lives. Now I know *that* house has to be avoided. And I continue the search, enjoy the very journey, the pilgrimage."

The insight in the story is tremendous. There are seekers of truth who have never thought, what will I do with truth? You cannot eat it, you cannot sell it; you cannot become a president because you have the truth. At the most, if you have the truth people will crucify you.

> ≫
> It is good that God is deaf. He does not hear prayers, otherwise you all will be in trouble.

He is right when he says, *My debts are large, my failures great, my shame secret and heavy. Yet when I come to ask for my good, I quake in fear lest my prayer be granted*—because these things are good to talk about: God, truth, good, beauty. It is good to write treatises about them, have universities confer Ph.D.s, let the Nobel committee give you a prize. It is good to talk and write about these things, but if you really get to experience them you will be in trouble. That's what he is saying: I am afraid that my prayer may be granted.

It is good that God is deaf. He does not hear prayers; otherwise you all will be in trouble. Your prayer will create your troubles, because in prayers you will be so romantic, asking great things which you cannot live by, which will become very heavy and will interfere in your so-called life—which is going on smoothly, although in misery.

Truth becomes a cross; life becomes heavy. Truth becomes poison to a Socrates. Truth becomes death to al-Hillaj Mansoor. Truth becomes crucifixion to Jesus Christ. And you pray, "God, give me truth. Give me qualities which are divine, godly." But God is deaf on purpose—so that your prayers cannot be heard and you can enjoy both, your miserable life and your beautiful prayers. The prayers will not be heard—you can remain jealous, angry, full of hate, full of egoism, and go on praying to God, "Make me humble; and because 'blessed are the meek,' make me meek"—but on purpose.

It is not written in any scripture, but I tell you on my personal authority that after creating the world in six days, the last thing God did was destroy his ears. Since then, we has never heard anything; and since then, neither have we heard anything about him.

So it is perfectly good: in the morning you go to the temple or the church or the mosque, have a beautiful prayer, ask great things—knowing perfectly well that he is deaf—and go on being your ugly, miserable self. Then tomorrow morning you do it again and have a good prayer. This is such a good arrangement.

Rabindranath in his poem is indicating a profound truth: Do you really want God? Do you really want truth? Do you really want silence? If you ask, and you are honest, you will feel ashamed. You will have to accept that you don't really want these things. You are only pretending to meditate—because you know you have been meditating for many years and nothing happens. There is no fear; you can meditate, nothing happens.

Once something starts happening, then there is trouble. Once something starts growing in your life that is not growing in the hearts of the crowd that surrounds you, you will be a stranger, you will be an outsider. And the crowd never forgives strangers, the crowd never forgives outsiders; it destroys them. It has to destroy them just for its own peace of mind.

A man like Jesus Christ is a continual nuisance, because he reminds you that you can also be of the same beauty, of the same grace, of the same truth, and it hurts. He makes you feel inferior, and nobody wants to feel inferior.

And there are only two ways not to feel inferior: one is to become superior; that is a hard way, and a long way—dangerous, because you will have to walk alone. The simpler way is, destroy that superior man. Then the whole crowd is made of equal people. Nobody is superior, nobody is inferior. All are cunning, all are cheats, all are criminals in their own way. All are jealous, all are ambitious. They are all in the same boat, and they understand each other's language. And nobody creates any fuss about truth, about God, about meditation.

People are happy without a Gautam Buddha, without a Socrates, without a Zarathustra, because these people are like high peaks of mountains and you look so tiny, like such pygmy, and it hurts. They say that camels never go near the mountains. They have chosen to live in the desert because in the desert they are the walking mountains, but near the mountains they will look like ants, and that hurts.

> The crowd never forgives strangers, the crowd never forgives outsiders, it destroys them. It has to destroy them just for its own peace of mind.

The easiest way is to forget all about mountains, to say, "These mountains are all mythological, fictitious; the reality is the desert." So you enjoy the desert, you enjoy your ego—and you also enjoy the prayer, "God, please free me of the ego, make me humble," knowing perfectly well that he does not hear, that no prayer is answered. You can pray for anything without fear because you will remain the same and you will also have the satisfaction of praying for great things.

> A religious person is simply religious; he is neither Hindu, nor Mohammedan, nor Christian, nor Buddhist—there is no need.

That's why people, without becoming religious, become Christians, become Hindus, become Mohammedans. They are not religious people at all; these are strategies to avoid being religious. A religious person is simply religious; he is neither Hindu, nor Mohammedan, nor Christian, nor Buddhist—there is no need. He is truthful, he is sincere, he is compassionate, he is loving, he is human—so human that he almost represents the divine in the world.

PATHS TO FREEDOM

A rebel is one who does not react against the society, who understands the whole game of it and simply slips out of it. It becomes irrelevant to him. He is not against it. And that is the beauty of rebellion: it is freedom. The revolutionary is not free. He is constantly fighting with something—how can he be free? He is constantly reacting against something—how can there be freedom in reaction?

Freedom means understanding. One has understood the game, and seeing that this is the way that the soul is prevented from growing, the way one is not allowed to be oneself, one simply gets out of it with no scar on the soul. One forgives and forgets and remains without any clinging to the society in the name of love or in the name of hate. Society has simply disappeared for the rebel. He may live in the world or he may go out of the world, but he belongs to it no more; he is an outsider.

CAMEL, LION, CHILD

Man is not born perfect. He is born incomplete. He is born as a process. He is born on the way, as a pilgrim. That is his agony and his ecstasy too—agony because he cannot rest, he has to go ahead, he has always to go ahead. He has to seek and search and explore; he has to become, because his being arises only through becoming. Becoming is his being. He can only be if he is on the move.

Evolution is intrinsic to man's nature, evolution is his very soul. And those who take themselves for granted remain unfulfilled; those who think they are born complete remain unevolved. Then the seed remains the seed, never becomes a tree, and never knows the joys of spring and the sunshine and the rain, and the ecstasy of bursting into millions of flowers.

> Evolution is intrinsic to man's nature, evolution is his very soul. And those who take themselves for granted remain unfulfilled, those who think they are born complete remain unevolved.

That explosion is the fulfillment, that explosion is what God is all about—exploding into millions of flowers. When the potential becomes the actual, only then is man fulfilled. Man is born as a potential; that is unique to man. All other animals are born complete, they are born as they are going to die. There is no evolution between their birth and their death: they move on the same plane, they never go through any transformation. No radical change in their life ever happens. They move horizontally; the vertical never penetrates them.

If man also moves horizontally he will miss his manhood, he will not become a soul. That's what Gurdjieff meant when he used to say that all people don't have souls. It is very rare that a person has a soul. Now this is a very strange statement, because down the ages you have been told that you are born with a soul. Gurdjieff says you are born only with the potential of becoming a soul, not with the actual soul. You have a blueprint, but the blueprint has to be worked out. You have the seed, but you have to search for the soil, and the season, and the right climate, and the right moment to explode, to grow.

Moving horizontally, you will remain without a soul. When the vertical penetrates you, you become a soul. "Soul" means the vertical has penetrated into the horizontal. Or, as an example, you can think of a caterpillar, the cocoon, and the butterfly.

Man is born as a larva. Unfortunately, many die also as larvae; very few become caterpillars. A larva is static: it knows no movement, it remains stuck at one space, at one place, at one stage. Very few people grow into caterpillars. The caterpillar starts moving; dynamism enters. The larva is static; the caterpillar moves. With movement life is stirred. Again, many remain caterpillars: they go on moving horizontally, on the same plane, in one dimension. Rarely, a man like Buddha—or Jalaluddin Rumi or Jesus or Kabir—takes the final quantum leap and becomes a butterfly. Then the vertical enters in.

The larva is static; the caterpillar moves, knows movement; the butterfly flies, knows heights, starts moving upwards. The butterfly grows wings; those wings are the goal. Unless you grow wings and you become a winged phenomenon, you will not have a soul.

Truth is realized through three states: assimilation, independence, and creativity. Remember these three words, they are very seminal. Assimilation—that is the function of the larva. It simply assimilates food; it is getting ready to become a caterpillar. It is arranging; it is a reservoir. When the energy is ready, it will become a caterpillar. Before the movement, you will need a great energy to move. The caterpillar is assimilation, complete; the work done.

Then the second stage starts: independence. The larva is dropped. Now there is no need to stay in one place. The time has come to explore, the time has come for the adventure. The real life starts with movement, independence. The larva remains dependent, a prisoner, in chains. The caterpillar has broken the chains, starts moving. The ice has melted; it is frozen no more. The larva is a frozen state. The caterpillar is movement, river-like.

And then comes the third stage, of creativity. Independence in itself does not mean much. Just by being independent you will not be fulfilled. It is good to be out of the prison, but for what? Independence for what? Freedom for what?

Remember, freedom has two aspects: first, freedom from, and second, freedom for. Many people attain only to the first kind of freedom, freedom from—free from the parents, free from the church, free from the organization, free from this and that, free from all kinds of prisons. But for what? This is a very negative freedom. If you know only freedom from, you have not known real freedom; you have known only the negative aspect. The positive has to be known—freedom to create, freedom to be, freedom to express, to sing your song, to dance your dance. That is the third state: creativity.

Then the caterpillar becomes a winged phenomenon, a honey-taster, searches, discovers, explores, creates. Hence, the beauty of the butterfly. Only creative people are beautiful because only creative people know the splendor of life: they have eyes to see and ears to hear and hearts to feel. They are fully alive; they live at the maximum. They burn their torch at both ends. They live in intensity; they live in totality.

Or, we can use the metaphors used by Friedrich Nietzsche. He says that man's life can be divided into three successive metamor-

> *Independence in itself does not mean much. Just by being independent you will not be fulfilled. It is good to be out of the prison, but for what? Independence for what? Freedom for what?*

phoses of the spirit. The first he calls "the camel," the second he calls "the lion" the third he calls "the child" Very pregnant metaphors—the camel, the lion and the child.

Each human being has to draw upon and assimilate the cultural heritage of his society—his culture, his religion, his people. He has to assimilate all that the past makes available. He has to assimilate the past; this is what Nietzsche calls the camel stage. The camel has the power of storing up in his body enormous amounts of food and water for his arduous journey across the desert. And it is the same for the human individual—you have to pass across a desert, you have to assimilate the whole past. And remember, just memorizing is not going to help . . . assimilation. And also remember: the person who memorizes the past memorizes only because he cannot assimilate. If you assimilate the past, you are free from the past. You can use it, but it cannot use you. You possess it, but it does not possess you.

When you have assimilated food you need not remember it. It does not exist separate from you: it has become your blood, your bone, your marrow; it has become you.

> The person who memorizes the past memorizes only because he cannot assimilate. If you assimilate the past you are free from the past. You can use it, but it cannot use you. You possess it, but it does not possess you.

The past has to be digested. Nothing is wrong with the past. It is your past. You need not begin from ABC, because if each individual had to begin from ABC there would not be much evolution. That's why animals have not evolved. The dog is the same as it was millions of years ago. Only man is the evolving animal. From where does this evolution come? It comes because man is the only animal who can assimilate the past. Once the past is assimilated you are free from it. You can move in freedom and you can use your past. Otherwise you will have to pass through so many experiences; your life will be wasted.

You can stand on the shoulders of your fathers and forefathers and their fathers and their forefathers. Man goes on standing upon each man's shoulders, hence the height that man achieves. Dogs cannot achieve that, wolves cannot achieve that; they depend on themselves. Their height is their height. In your height, Buddha is assimilated, Christ is assimilated, Patanjali is assimilated, Moses is assimilated, Lao Tzu is assimilated. The greater the assimilation the higher you stand. You can look from the peak of a mountain, your vision is great.

Assimilate more. There is no need to be confined by your own people. Assimilate the whole past of all the peoples of the whole earth; be a citizen of the planet earth. There is no need to be confined by the Christian and the Hindu and the Mohammedan. Assimilate all! The Koran is yours, the Bible is yours, so is the Talmud, and so are the Vedas and the Tao Te Ching—all is yours. Assimilate all, and the more you assimilate the higher will be the peak on which you can stand

> ✺
>
> The Koran is yours, the Bible is yours, so is the Talmud, and so are the Vedas and the Tao Te Ching— all is yours. Assimilate all, and the more you assimilate the higher will be the peak on which you can stand and look far away, and distant lands and distant views become yours.

and look far away, and distant lands and distant views become yours.

This Nietzsche calls the camel stage, but don't be stuck there. One has to move. The camel is the larva; the camel is a hoarder. But if you are stuck at that stage and always remain a camel, then you will not know the beauties and the benedictions of life. Then you will never know God. You will remain stuck in the past. The camel can assimilate the past but cannot use it.

In the course of his personal development the time comes when the camel has to become the lion. The lion proceeds to tear apart the huge monster known as "thou shalt not." The lion in man roars against all authority.

The lion is a reaction, a rebellion against the camel. The individual now discovers his own inner light as the ultimate source of all authentic values. He becomes aware of his primary obligation to his own inner creativity, to his inmost hidden potential. A few remain stuck at the stage of the lion: they go on roaring and roaring and become exhausted in their roaring.

It is good to become a lion, but one has still to take one more jump—and that jump is to become the child.

> Unless a man becomes utterly innocent, free from past, so free that he is not even against the past...Remember it, the person who is still against the past is not really free. He still has some grudges, some complaints, some wounds.

Now each of you has been a child. But those who know, they say the first childhood is a false childhood. It is like first teeth: they only look like teeth but they are of no use, they have to fall out. Then the real teeth are born. The first childhood is a false childhood; the second childhood is the real childhood. That second childhood is called the stage of the child or the stage of the sage— it means the same. Unless a man becomes utterly innocent, free from past, so free that he is not even against the past. . . . Remember it, the person who is still against the past is not really free. He still has some grudges, some complaints, some wounds. The camel still haunts him; the shadow of the camel still follows. The lion is there but still afraid somehow of the camel, fearful that it may come back.

When the fear of the camel is completely gone, the roaring of the lion stops. Then the song of the child is born.

I would like you to go into these three stages very deeply and very penetratingly, because they are of immense value.

The stage of the camel, assimilation, is just like a child in the womb who does nothing but assimilate, just eats the mother, gets bigger and bigger, is getting ready for the final plunge to move into the world. Right now there is no other work for the child: for nine months in the mother's womb he eats and sleeps, sleeps and eats. He goes on sleeping and eating; these are the only two functions. Even after the child is born, for months he will be doing just that— eating and sleeping. Slowly, slowly sleeping will become less and less and eating will also become less and less. He is ready, he is ready to become an individual—and the moment the child becomes ready to be an individual, disobedience enters in. The child starts saying no; yes-saying by and by disappears. Obedience dies; disobedience is born.

The state of the camel is the state of assimilation. The camel does not know how to say no. The camel is not acquainted with the no. He has not heard the word and he has not tasted the joys of saying no. He only knows yes. His yes cannot be very deep, because without knowing "no" your yes cannot be very deep; it has to remain superficial. The man who has not known no, how can he really know yes? His yes will be impotent. The camel's yes is impotent. The camel does not know what is happening; he only goes on saying yes because that is the only word that he has been taught. Obedience, belief—these are the characteristics of the stage called "camel." Adam was in this state before he ate the fruit of the Tree of Knowledge, and each human being passes through this state.

This is a state which is pre-mind and pre-self. There is no mind yet. The mind is growing but is not a complete phenomenon; it is very vague, ambiguous, dark, nebulous. The self is on the way but still is only on the way; there are no clear-cut definitions of it. The child does not know himself as separate yet. Adam, before he ate the fruit, was part of God. He was in the womb, he was obedient, a yea-sayer, but he was not independent. Independence enters only through the door of no; through the door of yes, only dependence. So in this stage of the camel, there is dependence, helplessness. The other is more important than your own being: God is more important, father is more important, mother is more important, society is more important, the priest is more important, the politician is more important. Except you, everybody is important; the *other* is important, you are still not there. It is a very unconscious state. The majority of the people are stuck there; they remain camels. Almost ninety-nine percent of people remain camels.

This is a very sad state of affairs—that ninety-nine percent of human beings remain as larvae. That's why there is so much misery and no joy. And you can go on searching for joy but you will not find it, because joy is not given there, outside. Unless you become a child—the third stage is attained—unless you become a butterfly, you will not be able to know joy. Joy is not something given outside; it is a vision that grows inside you. It is possible only in the third stage.

The first stage is of misery and the third stage is of bliss, and between the two is the state of the lion—which is sometimes miserable and sometimes pleasant, sometimes painful and sometimes pleasurable.

At the stage of the camel you are parrots. You are just memories, nothing else. Your whole life consists of beliefs given to you by others. This is where you will find the Christians and the Mohammedans and the Hindus and the Jainas and the Buddhists. Go into the churches and the temples and the mosques and you will find great gatherings of camels. You will not find a single human being. They go on repeating, parrot-like.

I have heard a story:

The story is told of the medieval knight who attended a course at the local dragon-slaying school. Several other young knights also attended this special class taught by Merlin, the magician.

Our antihero went to Merlin the first day to let him know that he would probably not do well in the course because he was a coward and was sure he would be much too frightened and inept ever to be able to slay a dragon. Merlin said he need not worry because there was a magic dragon-slaying sword which he would give this cowardly young knight. With such a sword in hand there was no way that anyone could fail in slaying any dragon. The knight was delighted to have this official magic prop with which any knight, no matter how worthless, could kill a dragon. From the first field trip on, magic sword in hand, the cowardly knight slew dragon after dragon, freeing one maiden after another.

One day, toward the end of the term, Merlin sprung a pop quiz on the class which the young knight was attending. The students were to go out in the field and kill a dragon that very day. In the flurry of excitement as all the young knights rushed off to prove their mettle, our anti-hero grabbed the wrong sword from the rack. Soon he found himself at the mouth of a cave from which he was to free a bound maiden. Her fire-breathing captor came rushing out. Not knowing that he had picked the wrong weapon, the young knight drew back his sword in preparation for undoing the charging dragon. As he was about to strike he noticed that he had taken the wrong sword. No magic sword this, just your ordinary adequate-for-good-knights-only sword.

It was too late to stop. He brought down the ordinary sword with a trained sweep of his arm, and to his surprise and delight, off came the head of still another dragon.

Returning to the class, dragon's head tied to his belt, sword in hand, and maiden in tow, he rushed to tell Merlin of his mistake and of his unexplainable recovery.

Merlin laughed when he heard the young knight's story. His answer to the young knight was, "I thought that you would have guessed by now: none of the swords are magic and none of them ever have been. The only magic is in the believing."

The camel lives in the magic of believing. It works. It can work miracles. But the camel remains a camel; the growth is missing.

The people praying in the temples and the churches are under the influence of belief. They don't know what God is, they have never felt anything like that; they only believe. Their magic of belief goes on doing certain things to them, but that is all make-believe, a kind of dreamworld. They are not out of the unconscious, out of their sleep. And remember, I am not saying that this stage is not necessary; it is necessary, but once it is complete one has to jump out of it. One is not here to remain a camel forever.

And don't be angry at your parents, or teachers, or priests, or society, because they HAVE to create a kind of obedience in you—because only through obedience will you be able to assimilate. The father has to teach, the mother has to teach, and the child has to simply absorb. If doubt arises prematurely, assimilation will be stopped.

Just think of a child in the mother's womb who becomes doubtful—he will die—becomes doubtful of whether to partake of food from this woman or not, whether the food is really nourishing or not: "Who knows, it may be poisonous?"—whether to sleep for twenty-four hours or not, because this is too much, sleeping continuously for twenty-four hours, for nine months. If the child becomes a little bit doubtful, in that very doubt the child will die. And still, a day comes when doubt has to be imbibed, learned. Each thing has its own season.

> Don't be angry at your parents, or the teachers, or the priests, or the society, because they *have* to create a kind of obedience in you—because only through obedience will you be able to assimilate.

Each father is faced with the problem: what to tell the son? Each mother confronts the problem: what to teach the daughter? Every teacher worries: what should be imparted to the new generation? The past has much, many glories, many peaks of understanding, many conclusions which have to be imparted to the child.

In the first stage everybody has to be a camel, yea-saying, believing whatsoever is given, assimilating, digesting, but this is only the beginning of the journey; this is not the end.

The second stage is difficult. The first stage society gives you;

that's why there are millions of camels and very few lions. Society
leaves you when you have become a perfect camel. Beyond that, society cannot do anything. It is there that the work of society
ends—the society of the school, the college, the university. It leaves
you a perfect camel with a certificate.

A lion you have to become on your own—remember it. If you
don't decide to become a lion, you will never become a lion. That
risk has to be taken by the individual. That is a gamble. That is very
dangerous too, because by becoming a lion you will annoy all the
camels around you, and the camels are peace-loving animals; they
are always ready to compromise. They don't want to be disturbed,
they don't want any new thing to happen in the world, because all
new things disturb. They are against the revolutionaries and the rebellious, and not about great things, mind you—not about Socrates
and Christ; they are bringing great revolutions—the camels are
afraid of such small things that you will be surprised.

I have heard:

In December, 1842, Adam Thompson of Cincinnati filled
the first bathtub in the United States. The news of Mr.
Thompson's tub was quickly spread. Newspapers said that
the newfangled idea would ruin the democratic simplicity
of the republic.

Mm, just think of it . . . a bathtub will ruin the in-
tegrity of the democratic republic.

. . . Doctors predicted rheumatism, inflammation of
the lungs, etc. The wise ones agreed that bathing in the
wintertime would result in the decline of the robust population. Philadelphia, the cradle of liberty, tried to put a
ban on bathing from the first of November to the first of
March; Boston in 1845 made bathing unlawful except on
the advice of a doctor; Hartford, Providence, Wilmington,

and other cities tried to block the bath habit with extra heavy water rates. The state of Virginia took a slap at bathing by placing a tax of thirty dollars a year on every bathtub brought into the state. But by 1922, 889,000 bathtubs were manufactured a year.

The camels are simply against *anything* new; it does not matter what. It may be just a bathtub, and they will rationalize their antagonism.

In one section of ancient Greece it was long the custom that when a man proposed a new law in the popular assembly, he did so on a platform with a rope around his neck. If the law was passed they removed the rope; if it failed they removed the platform.

The lions are not welcome. The society creates every kind of difficulty for the lions. The camels are afraid of these people. They disturb their convenience, they disturb their sleep, they create worry. They create a desire in the camels to become lions—that is the real problem.

Why is Jesus crucified? His very presence . . . and many camels start dreaming of becoming lions, and that disturbs their sleep, and that disturbs their ordinary, mundane life.

Why is Buddha stoned? Why is Mahavira not allowed to enter into cities? Why is Mansoor beheaded? These people disturb; they disturb their sleep, they go on roaring. Buddha has called his sermons "The Lion's Roar."

The first, the state of the camel, is given by the society. The second state has to be attained by the individual. In attaining it, you become an individual, you become unique. You are no more a conformist, you are no more part of a tradition. The cocoon is dropped: you become a caterpillar, you start moving.

The state of the lion has these characteristics: independence, no-saying, disobedience, rebellion against the other, against authority, against dogma, against scripture, against the church, against the political power, against the state. The lion is against everything! He wants to shatter everything and create the whole world anew, closer to the heart's desire. He has great dreams and utopias in his mind. He looks mad to the camels, because the camels live in the past and the lion starts living in the future. A great gap arises. The lion heralds the future, and the future can come only if the past is destroyed. The new can enter into existence only if the old ceases to exist and creates space for the new. The old has to die for the new to be. So there is a constant fight between the lion and the camel, and the camels are the majority. The lion happens once in a while, the lion is an exception—and the exception only proves the rule.

Disbelief is his characteristic, doubt is his characteristic. Adam eats the fruit of the Tree of Knowledge: mind is born, self becomes a defined phenomenon. The camel is non-egoistic; the lion is very egoistic. The camel knows nothing of the ego; the lion only knows the ego. That's why you will always find revolutionaries, rebellious people—poets, painters, musicians—are all very egoistic. They are bohemians. They live their life, they do *their* thing. They don't care a bit about others. Let the others go to hell! They are no more a part of any structure, they become free from the structures. The movement, the lion's roar, is bound to be egoistic. They need a great ego to go into this.

> The lion is against everything! He wants to shatter everything and create the whole world anew, closer to the heart's desire. He has great dreams and utopias in his mind.

In the East you will find more camels; in the West you will find more lions. That's why in the East to surrender seems so easy. For the Western mind surrender seems so difficult. But one thing has to be remembered: the Eastern mind finds it very easy to surrender;

that's why his surrender is not of much value. He's already surrendered. He does not know how to say no; that's why he says yes. When a Western mind surrenders it is very difficult. It is a struggle for the Western mind to surrender, but when the Western mind surrenders there is great transformation, because the surrender has been hard, arduous, an uphill task. In the East the surrender is cheap; in the West it is costly. Only a few courageous people can afford it.

> Each individual has to be taught the ego before he will be able to drop it. Each individual has to come to a very crystallized ego, only then is the dropping of any help, otherwise not.

The East surrenders because there is no more possibility of becoming a lion. It feels very comfortable, easy to surrender, to become part of a mob, a mass. The West has created the ego. The West has paid more attention to the lion—doubt, disbelief, ego—but whenever the Western mind surrenders, there is really great transformation.

The Eastern mind surrenders, remains the camel. If the Western mind surrenders there is a possibility for the "child" to be born. When the lion surrenders he becomes the child; when the camel surrenders he remains the camel.

So I may appear paradoxical to you, but if you understand what I am saying it will not be very difficult and the paradox will not really look like a paradox. Each individual has to be taught the ego before he will be able to drop it. Each individual has to come to a very crystallized ego; only then is the dropping of any help, otherwise not.

The first state, of the camel, is unconscious. The second state, of the lion, is subconscious—a little higher than the unconscious. A few glimpses of the conscious have started coming in. The sun is rising, and a few rays are entering into the dark room where you are asleep. The unconscious is no more unconscious. Something is stirred in the unconscious; it has become subconscious. But remember, the change is not very great—from the camel to the lion—as it is going to be from the lion to the child. The change is a kind of reversion. The camel starts standing on its head and becomes the lion. The camel says yes, the lion says no. The camel obeys, the lion disobeys. The camel is positive, the lion is negative. It is to be understood that the camel has been saying yes so much and must have been denying the no—the no accumulates; and a point comes where the no wants to take revenge on the yes. The denied part wants to take revenge. Then the whole wheel turns—the camel turns upside-down and becomes the lion.

The difference between the camel and the lion is big, but both exist on the same plane. The cocoon is static at one place; the caterpillar starts moving, but on the same earth. Movement is born but the plane is the same. The first thing is given by the society: your being a camel is a gift of the society. Your being a lion will be a gift that you give to yourself. Unless you love yourself you will not be able to do it. Unless you want to become an individual, unique in your own right, unless you take the risk of going against the current, you will not be able to become a lion.

But if you understand the mechanism . . . in the very heart of the camel the lion is created. Again and again, saying yes and denying no, no goes on accumulating. And one day comes when one is fed up with saying yes; just for the change one wants to say no. One is fed up with the positive, the taste of it becomes monotonous; just for the change one wants to taste no.

That's how the camel, for the first time, starts having dreams of the lion. And once you have tasted the no—the doubt, the disbelief—you can never be a camel again, because it brings such liberty, such freedom.

The majority is stuck at the camel stage, the minority is stuck at the lion stage. The majority means the masses, and the minority means the intelligentsia. The artist, the poet, the painter, the musician, the thinker, the philosopher, the revolutionary—they are stuck at the second stage. They are far better than the camels, but the goal is not yet achieved. They have not come home. The third stage is "the child."

Listen attentively: the first stage is given by the society, the second is given by the individual to himself. The third is possible only if the caterpillar comes close by to a butterfly; otherwise it is not possible. How will the caterpillar ever think that he can fly on his own, that he can become a winged thing? It is not possible! It is impossible to think! It will be absurd, illogical. The caterpillar knows how to move, but to fly is just absurd.

I have heard about butterflies teaching the caterpillars that they can fly, and they object and they say, "No. It may be possible for you, but it is not possible for us. You are a butterfly, we are only caterpillars! We only know how to crawl." And one who knows only how to crawl, how can he imagine flying? That is a different dimension, an altogether different dimension—the vertical dimension.

From the camel to the lion, it is evolution. From the lion to the child, it is revolution. A Master is needed at that stage. The society can make you a camel, you yourself can make yourself a lion, but you will need a Master—a Buddha, a Christ, a Rumi—you will need a butterfly who has wings. Only with a winged phenomenon will you be able to start dreaming about wings. How can you dream about something that you have not known at all? Do you think that a very primitive tribe living somewhere in the Himalayas can dream of a car? They have not seen one; they cannot dream about it. The dream is possible only when you have seen something—when you have seen a Christ or a Buddha or a Bodhidharma, and you know that this happens. And these people look just like you, and still they are not like you. They have the same body, the same structure, and yet something from the unknown has penetrated their being. The beyond has come into them, the beyond is very very tangible there. If you approach them with sympathy and love, you will be able to have a few glimpses of their inner sky. And once you have seen that inner sky you will start dreaming about it. A great longing will arise in you: how to become a winged phenomenon?

That is the infection that comes from the Master to the disciple. The third phenomenon happens through the Master. "The child" means creativity, interdependence.

The first stage, the camel, was dependence; the second stage was independence; but in innocence one comes to know that neither is there dependence nor is there independence. Existence is interdependence—all are dependent on each other. It is all one.

The sense of the whole is born: no I, no thou, no fixation with yes or no, no obsession either to say yes always or to say no always; more fluidity, more spontaneity; neither obedience nor disobedience, but spontaneity. Responsibility is born. One responds to existence, does not react out of the past, and does not react out of the future.

> In innocence one comes to know that neither is there dependence nor is there independence. Existence is interdependence—all are dependent on each other. It is all one.

The camel lives in the past, the lion lives in the future, the child lives in the present, here-now. The camel is pre-mind, the lion is mind, the child is post-mind. The camel is pre-self, the lion is self, the child is post-self. That's what the meaning of the state of no-mind is. Sufis call it *fana*—the ego is gone, the other too. They are both together, you cannot have one without the other. I-thou are part of one energy; they both disappear.

The child simply is . . . ineffable, indefinable, a mystery, a wonder. The camel has memory, the lion has knowledgeability and the child has wisdom. The camel is either Christian, Hindu, or Mohammedan, theist, the lion is atheist, and the child is religious—neither theist nor atheist, neither Hindu nor Mohammedan nor Christian nor communist; just a simple religiousness, the quality of love and innocence.

Adam eats the fruit, becomes a lion. Adam, before eating the fruit from the Tree of Knowledge, is the camel. And when Adam has vomited the fruit again, dropped knowledge, he is the child. That child means Christ. Christ says again and again to his disciples, "Repent!" The word "repent" in Hebrew means return, go back; the Garden of Eden is still waiting for you. Vomit this apple of knowledge and the doors will be opened unto you.

The camel is Adam before eating the fruit, the lion is Adam after eating the fruit, and the child is Adam become Christ, returning back home. Buddha calls it *Nirvana,* Jesus calls it the Kingdom of God. You can call it anything you like: Tao, *dhamma, moksha.* Words don't mean much there; it is a wordless silence, a thoughtless innocence.

FROM LOVE TO LOVINGNESS

The word *love* can have two absolutely different meanings—not only different, but diametrically opposite. One meaning is love as relationship; the other meaning is love as a state of being. The moment love becomes a relationship it becomes a bondage, because there are expectations and there are demands and there are frustrations, and an effort from both sides to dominate. It becomes a struggle for power. Relationship is not the right thing. But love as a state of being is totally different. It means you are simply loving; you are not creating a relationship out of it. Your love is just like the fragrance of a flower. It does not create a relationship; it does not ask you to be a certain way, to behave in a certain way, to act in a certain way. It demands nothing. It simply shares. And in sharing also there is no desire for any reward. The sharing itself is the reward.

When love becomes like a fragrance to you, then it has tremendous beauty. And something that is far above the so-called humanity—it has something of the divine.

When love is a state, you cannot do anything about it. It will radiate but it will not create any imprisonments for anybody, nor will it allow you to be imprisoned by anybody else.

But you are accustomed to creating relationships, from your very childhood. A strange man, and you have to create a relationship with him as your father. You cannot ever be certain that he really is your father . . .

> Love is just like the fragrance of a flower. It does not create a relationship, it does not ask you to be a certain way, to behave in a certain way, to act in a certain way. It demands nothing. It simply shares.

I have heard about a palmist who used to read people's hands. An atheist, a young man who did not believe in God and did not believe in any kind of bullshit—palmistry, astrology—went to this palmist and said, "If your science is true, just read my hand and tell me where my father is right now."

The palmist looked at his hand and said, "Your father has gone fishing." The atheist laughed. He said, "That's what I say: it is all nonsense. My father has been dead for three years; how can he go fishing today?"

The palmist said, "That is not my business, but the truth is, the man who died was not your father. Your real father is fishing. You go to your mother and ask. If she is sincere and honest, she will tell you that the man who died was not your father—although you had created a relationship because you were told that he is your father."

Your whole life is surrounded by many kinds of relationships. And relationship as such, real or imaginary, is a very subtle kind of psychological slavery. Either you enslave the other, or you become a slave yourself.

Another point to be noted is that you cannot enslave somebody without becoming a slave yourself. Slavery is a double-edged sword. One may be stronger, one may be weaker, but in every relationship you become the jailer and the other becomes the prisoner. From his side, he is the jailer and you are the prisoner. And this is one of the fundamental causes of humanity living in such sadness, in such a sorrowful state.

And hate is much stronger a relationship than your love, because your love is very superficial. Your hate is very deep. Your hate is your whole animal heritage. Your love is only a potential for the future; it is not an actuality, but only a seed. But your hate is full-fledged, fully grown—thousands of years of your past moving through different life forms. It has had time and space to grow. It is only in man that the change starts happening.

But I cannot prevent anybody from hating me, so how can I prevent anybody from loving me? All that I can do is to explain that the moment hate or love or anything becomes a relationship, it loses its purity.

Let your love be your state of being. Not that you fall in love, but just that you are loving. It is simply your nature. Love, to you, is just the fragrance of your being. Even if you are alone you are surrounded by loving energy. Even if you touch a dead thing, like a chair, your hand is showering love—it does not matter to whom or what. The loving state is unaddressed.

I am not suggesting that you should not be in a state of love, but you can be in a state of love only if you drop the old mind pattern of relationships. Love is not a relationship.

Two persons can be very loving together. The more loving they are, the less is the possibility of any relationship. The more loving they are, the more freedom exists between them. The more loving they are, the less is the possibility of any demand, any domination, any expectation. And naturally, there is no question of any frustration.

When two persons are in a relationship and their expectations are not fulfilled—and they are not going to be fulfilled—then immediately love turns into hate. Expectations were there; now frustrations are there—but first they were projecting their expectations; now they are projecting their frustrations. Neither can see that they are surrounded with their own unconscious ideas. And they are suffering.

> Let your love be your state of being. Not that you fall in love, but just that you are loving. It is simply your nature.

And, just as when they were imagining love, they were appreciating the other, not knowing the other at all, now they are condemning the other. That's why I want you to remember: don't have any expectations. Love because love is your own inner growth. Your love will help you to grow toward more light, toward more truth, toward more freedom. But don't create a relationship.

Just remember one thing: love is capable of destroying everything else, just don't let it become a relationship—then love will disappear, and in the name of love, domination, politics will take place. Then problems will go on increasing.

I am against all kinds of relationships. For example, I don't like the word "friendship," but I love the word "friendliness." Friendliness is a quality in you, friendship again becomes a relationship.

So there is nothing wrong with love. In fact, without love everything is wrong. But love is so valuable that it should be protected from any kind of pollution, contamination, any kind of poisoning. Relationship poisons it. I want the world to consist of individuals. Even to use the word "couple" hurts me. You have destroyed two individuals, and a couple is not a thing of beauty.

Let the world be only of individuals, and whenever love spontaneously blossoms, sing it, dance it, live it; don't create chains out of it. Neither try to hold somebody in bondage, nor allow anybody to hold you in bondage.

A world consisting only of free individuals will be a truly free world.

It is one of the greatest needs of man to be needed. Hence I cannot conceive of any time when love will not be in existence. As long as there are human beings, love will remain their most cherished experience. It is something that is available on the earth but does not belong to the earth. It gives you wings to fly like an eagle across the sun.

Without love you are without wings. But because it is such a nourishment and such a need, all the problems have arisen around it. You want your lover or your beloved to be available to you tomorrow too. It has been beautiful today, and you are worried about tomorrow. Hence marriage came into existence. It is just the fear that perhaps tomorrow your lover or your beloved may leave you—so make it a contract in front of society and in front of the law. But it is ugly—it is absolutely ugly, disgusting. To make love a contract means you are putting law above love; it means you are putting the collective mass above your individuality and you are taking the support of the courts, of the armies, of the police, of the judges, to make your bondage absolutely certain and safe. Tomorrow morning . . . one never knows. Love comes like a breeze—it may come again, it may not come. And when it does not come, then just because of the law, because of marriage, because of a concern for social respectability, almost all the couples in the world are reduced to prostitution.

Living with a woman that you don't love, living with a man that you don't love, living for safety, living for security, living for financial support, living together for any reason except love, makes it nothing but prostitution. I would like prostitution to disappear completely from the world. All the religions have been saying that there should be no prostitution—but this is how human stupidity works. These same religions that say there to be no prostitution are the causes of prostitution, because on the one hand they support marriage and on the other hand they are against prostitution.

Marriage itself *is* a prostitution. If I trust my love, why should I get married? The very idea of getting married is a sign of distrust. And something that comes out of distrust is not going to help your love grow deeper and higher. It is going to destroy it. Love, but don't destroy love by something fake—marriage or any other kind of relationship. Love is authentic only when it gives freedom. Let this be the criterion. Love is true only when it does not interfere in the privacy of the other person. It respects his individuality, his privacy. But the lovers that you see around the world, their whole effort is that nothing should be private; all secrets should be told to them. They are afraid of individuality; they destroy each other's individuality and they hope that by destroying each other, their lives will become a contentment, a fulfillment. They simply become more and more miserable.

Be loving, and remember that anything real is always changing. You have been given wrong notions that a true love remains forever. A true rose flower does not remain forever. A living being himself has to die one day. Existence is a constant change. But the notion, the idea that love should be permanent if it is true . . . and if love disappears one day, then the natural corollary is that it was not true love.

> Flowers are going to come forever, but don't cling to one flower. Otherwise soon you will be clinging to a dead flower. And that's what the reality is: people are clinging to a dead love that once was alive. Now it is only a memory and a pain and you are stuck because of your concern about respectability, because of the law.

The truth is that love came suddenly; it was not because of any effort on your part. It came as a gift of nature. When it came, you would not have accepted it if you had been worried about its going suddenly one day. The way it comes, it goes. But there is no need to be worried, because if one flower has faded, other flowers will be coming. Flowers are going to come forever, but don't cling to one flower. Otherwise soon you will be clinging to a dead flower. And that's what the reality is: people are clinging to a dead love that once was alive. Now it is only a memory and a pain and you are stuck because of your concern about respectability, because of the law.

Karl Marx had the idea, the right idea, that in communism there would be no marriages. And when the revolution happened in Russia, in the first four, five years they tried to make love a freedom. But then they became aware of practical difficulties of which Marx was not aware—he was only theorizing—and the greatest difficulty was that if there is no marriage, the family disappears. And the family is the backbone, the very spine of the society, of the nation. If the family disappears, then the nation cannot last long.

Within just five years after the revolution the communist party of Russia changed the whole idea. Marriage was again supported; divorce was allowed, but very reluctantly—every obstacle was created for divorce, so that the family unit could remain, because now they were interested in strengthening the nation. Without the nation there would be no politicians, there would be no government. And after that, they never talked about the fact that one of Marx's fundamental ideas was that marriage came into existence because of private property, so when private property disappears, marriage also has to disappear. Nobody talked about it.

I don't want the family to exist, I don't want nations to exist—I don't want the world to be divided into parts. I want one world consisting of free individuals living in spontaneous love, living in silence, playfulness, without any condemnation of pleasure, without any fear of hell and without any desire for reward in heaven—because we can create the paradise here. We have every potential to create it, but we are not using it. On the contrary, we are creating every hindrance.

I am not against love. I am so much in favor of love; that's why I am against relationships, against marriages. It is possible that two persons may live their whole lives together. Nobody is saying that you have to separate, but this living together will be only out of love, without interfering and trespassing into each other's individuality, into each other's private soul. That is the other person's dignity.

You can be loving, you can *be* love. And if you are simply loving, if you are simply love, then there is no possibility of that love turning into hate. Because there is no expectation, you cannot be frustrated. But I am talking about love as a spiritual phenomenon, not as biology. Biology is not love, it is lust. Biology is interested in continuing the species; the idea of love is just a biological bribe.

The moment you have made love to a woman or to a man, suddenly you find you are no longer interested, at least for twenty-four hours. And it depends on your age—as you become older, forty-eight hours, seventy-two hours . . .

There is a new commander of a base of the French Foreign Legion, and the captain is showing him around all the buildings. After he has made the rounds, the commander looks at the captain and says, "Wait a minute. You haven't shown me that small blue building over there. What's that used for?"

The captain says, "Well, sir, you see, that is where we keep the camel. Whenever the men feel the need for a woman . . ."

"Enough!" says the commander in disgust.

Well, two weeks later, the commander himself starts to feel in need of a woman. He goes to the captain and says, "Tell me something, captain." Lowering his voice and glancing furtively around, he asks, "Is the camel free anytime soon?"

The captain says, "Well, let me see." He opens up his book. "Why, yes, sir, the camel is free tomorrow afternoon at two o'clock."

The commander says, "Put me down."

So the next day at two o'clock the commander goes to the little blue building and opens the door. Inside he finds the cutest camel he has ever seen. He closes the door.

The captain hears a great roaring and screaming, so he runs up and bursts into the hut. He finds the commander naked, covered in camel hair and mud.

"Ahem, begging your pardon, sir," says the captain, "but wouldn't it be wiser to do as all the other men do—ride the camel into town and find a woman?"

FROM REACTION TO ACTION

The first thing, and the most basic to be understood, is that whatsoever you do, it should not be a reaction. If it is an *act* then there is no problem. *Action* is always good; *reaction* always bad.

So try first to understand the term *reaction*. It means you are acting unconsciously. Somebody is manipulating you. Somebody says something, does something, and you react. The real master of the situation is somebody else. Somebody comes and insults you and you react, you become angry. Somebody comes and praises you and you smile and you become happy. Both are the same. You are a slave and the other knows how to push your buttons. You are behaving like a machine. You are an automaton, not a human being yet.

Act, don't react. Don't be a plaything in the hands of others.

And you cannot predict a person who acts out of no-mind. Only mind is predictable. If you are awake, alert, conscious, no one can say what turn any situation will take. A thousand and one alternatives open for consciousness. Consciousness is total freedom—spontaneous, an *act*, totally in the present, not controlled by anybody else, coming out of one's own being . . .

We react according to our conditionings. If you have been born into a vegetarian family and nonvegetarian food is placed on your table, you will feel nauseated and sick—not because of the nonvegetarian food, but because of your conditioning. Somebody else who has been conditioned to eat meat will relish the very sight of it, will feel appetite not nausea, will feel happy, will be thrilled. That too is a conditioning.

We react because we have been conditioned in a certain way. You can be conditioned to be very polite. You can be conditioned to be always in control. You can be conditioned to be silent. You can be conditioned to remain still in situations where people ordinarily become disturbed and distracted. But if it is conditioning, then it has nothing to do with religiousness; then it has something to do with psychology. And a Buddha or a Jesus are not the masters there—B. F. Skinner and Pavlov, they are the masters there. It is a conditioned reflex.

I have heard the story that a new mouse was introduced in B. F. Skinner's lab.

Psychologists go on working with mice because they don't give any more credit than that to man. They think that if they can understand the mind of a mouse, they have understood humanity.

> ❧
> Psychologists go on working with mice because they don't give any more credit than that to man. They think that if they can understand the mind of a mouse, they have understood humanity.

The old mouse, who had been there with Skinner for a very long time, initiated the new one and said, "Look. This B. F. Skinner is a good man, but you have to condition him first. Push this button and immediately your breakfast comes in. I have conditioned him perfectly."

Conditioning is murder; your spontaneity is killed. The mind is fed with certain ideas and you are not allowed to respond; you are only allowed to react. In small things or great things, it is the same.

If you have been brought up in a religious family, the word *God* is beautiful, so holy. But if you have been brought up in a communist family, then the very word is ugly, nauseating. One feels that to utter the word would leave a bad taste in the mouth.

Small or large is not the question. If you go on behaving the way you have been conditioned, you are functioning as a machine; the human has not been born yet.

It is said that when you tell an Englishman a joke, he will laugh three times. He will laugh the first time—when you tell it—to be polite. He will laugh a second time—when you explain it—again to be polite. That is the training of the Englishman—to always be polite. Finally, he will laugh a third time in the middle of the night when he wakes from a sound sleep and suddenly gets it.

When you tell a German the same joke, he will laugh twice. He will laugh first—when you tell it—to be polite. He will laugh a second time—when you explain it—to be polite. He will never laugh a third time, because he will never get it.

When you tell an American the same joke, he will laugh once—when you tell it—because he will get it.

And when you tell a Jew the same joke, he won't laugh at all. Instead he will say, "It's an old joke, and besides, you are telling it all wrong."

It may be a joke, or it may be a great philosophy. It may be trivia or God himself, it makes no difference. People behave the way they are conditioned to behave, the way they are brought up to behave, the way they are expected to behave. Nature is not allowed to function; only nurture is allowed to function. These are the people whom I call slaves.

When you become free, when you drop all conditioning and for the first time look at life with fresh eyes, with no clouds of conditioning in between, then you become unpredictable. Then nobody knows, then nobody can imagine what is going to happen. Because then *you* are no longer there; existence acts through you. Right now only the society goes on acting through you.

Once you are simply alert, ready to respond, with no fixed idea, with no prejudice, with no plan, whatsoever happens in the moment, you become true and authentic.

Remember two words: authority and authenticity. Ordinarily you behave according to the authority that has conditioned you— the priest, the politician, the parents. You behave according to the authority. A man of freedom does not behave according to the authority; he behaves through his own authenticity. He responds. A situation arises, a challenge is there—and he responds with his total being. Even he himself cannot predict it.

When you ask me a question, even I don't know what answer I am going to give you. When I give it, only then I know; only then I say, "So, this was the answer!" Your question is there, I am here—a response is bound to happen.

Response is responsibility. Response is authenticity. Response is living in the moment.

You can always predict what unconscious people will do: they will be brave or they will be cowards, they will be patient or they will be impatient. But for an individual of understanding there are no "either/or" alternatives—all possibilities are always open; no door is closed. And each moment decides. The conscious individual, the free individual, does not carry a decision beforehand; he has no ready-made decisions. Fresh, virgin, he moves. He is uncorrupted by the past.

Awareness is the key. If you become aware, everything follows.

> Once you are
> simply alert,
> ready to respond,
> with no fixed idea,
> with no prejudice,
> with no plan,
> whatsoever happens
> in the moment, you
> become true
> and authentic.

Don't try to become anything—patient, loving, n
peaceful. Don't try. If you try, you will force yourself and you w
become a hypocrite. That's how the whole of religion has turned
into hypocrisy. Inside you are different; on the outside you are
painted. You smile, and inside you would have liked to kill. Inside
you carry all the rubbish and on the outside you go on sprinkling
perfume. Inside you stink; on the outside you create the illusion of
a rose.

<u>Never repress anything.</u> Repression is the greatest calamity that has happened to man. And it has happened for very beautiful reasons. You look at a Buddha—so silent, undisturbed. Greed arises: you would also like to be like that. What to do? You start trying to be a stone statue. Whenever there is a situation and you can be disturbed, you hold yourself back. You control yourself.

Control is a dirty word. It has more than four letters in it, but it is a four-letter word.

Freedom . . . And when I say freedom I don't mean license. You may misunderstand. When I say freedom you may understand it to mean license, because that's how

> Don't try to become anything—patient, loving, nonviolent, peaceful. Don't try. If you try, you will force yourself and you will become a hypocrite. That's how the whole of religion has turned into hypocrisy.

things go. A controlled mind, whenever it hears about freedom, immediately understands it as license. License is the opposite pole of control. Freedom is just in between, exactly in the middle, where there is no control and no license.

Freedom has its own discipline, but it is not enforced by any authority. It comes out of your awareness, out of authenticity. Freedom should never be misunderstood as license, otherwise you will again miss the point.

Awareness brings freedom. In freedom there is no need for control because there is no possibility for license. It is because of license that you have been forced to control, and if you remain licentious society will go on controlling you.

It is because of your licentiousness that the policeman exists, and the judge and the politician and the courts, and they go on forcing you to control yourself. And in controlling yourself you miss the whole point of being alive, because you miss celebration. How can you celebrate if you are too controlled?

It happens almost every day. When people come to see me who are very controlled and disciplined, it is almost impossible to penetrate their skulls; they are too thick . . . walls of stone are around them. They have become stony; they have become ice-cold; their warmth is lost. Because if you are warm, there is fear—you may do something. So they have killed themselves, completely poisoned themselves. To remain in control, they have found only one solution and that is not to live at all. So be a stone Buddha—then you will be able to pretend that you are patient, silent, disciplined.

But that is not what I am teaching here. Control needs to be

> ❧
>
> You can say, "If I drop control, I will become licentious. If I drop license then I have to become controlled." But I tell you, if you become aware, control and license both go down the same drain. They are two aspects of the same coin, and in awareness they are not needed.

dropped as much as license. Now, you will be puzzled. You can choose either control or license—you can say, "If I drop control, I will become licentious. If I drop license, then I have to become controlled." But I tell you, if you become aware, control and license both go down the same drain. They are two aspects of the same coin, and in awareness they are not needed.

It happened:

An eighteen year-old boy, who had always been somewhat shy and retiring, one evening decided to change himself. He came down from his bedroom all slicked up, and snapped at his father, "Look, I'm going out on the town— I'm going to find some beautiful girls. I'm going to get blind drunk and have a great time. I'm going to do all the things a fellow of my age should be doing in the prime of life and get a bit of adventure and excitement, so just don't try and stop me!"

His old man said, "Try and stop you? Hold on, son, I'm coming with you!"

All controlled people are in that state—bubbling inside, waiting to explode into licentiousness.

Go and see your monks in the monasteries. In India that type of neurosis is everywhere. The monks are all neurotics. This is something to be understood: either you become erotic or you become neurotic. If you repress your eros, your eroticism, you become neurotic. If you drop your neurosis, you become erotic. And both are types of madness. One should be simply oneself—neither neurotic nor erotic, available to all situations, ready to face whatever life brings, ready to accept and live—but always alert, conscious, aware, mindful.

So the only thing to be constantly remembered is self-remembrance. You should not forget yourself. And always move from the innermost core of your being. <u>Let actions flow from there, from your very center of being</u>, and whatever you do will be virtuous.

Virtue is a function of awareness.

If you do something from the periphery, it may not look like a sin, but it is sin. Society may be happy with you, but you cannot be happy with yourself. Society may praise you, but you deep down will go on condemning yourself because you will know you have missed life—and missed it for nothing.

<u>Of what value is the praise of the society?</u> If people call you a saint, what does it mean? It is nothing but gossip. How does it matter? You have missed godliness for gossip! You have missed life for these foolish people who are all around, for the sake of their good opinion.

Live life from your very center. This is all that meditation is about. And by and by you will come to feel a discipline that is not forced, not cultivated, which arises spontaneously, arises naturally like a flower blooms. <u>Then you will have the whole of life available, and you will have your whole being available.</u>

And when your whole being and the whole life meet, between the two arises that which is freedom. Between the two arises that which is nirvana.

REBELLION NOT REVOLUTION

Man has not come to the point where governments can be dissolved. Anarchists like Kropotkin have been against the government, the law. He wanted to dissolve them. I am also an anarchist, but in a totally opposite way to Kropotkin.

I want to raise the consciousness of human beings to the point where government becomes futile, courts remain empty, nobody is murdered, nobody is raped, nobody is tortured or harassed. Do you see the difference? Kropotkin's emphasis is to dissolve the governments. My emphasis is to raise the consciousness of human beings to the point where governments become, of their own accord, useless; to the point that courts start closing, that police start disappearing because there is no work and judges are told, "Find some other job." I am an anarchist from a very different dimension. First let people be ready, and governments will disappear on their own. I am not in favor of destroying governments; they are fulfilling a certain need. Man is so barbarous, so ugly, that if he is not prevented by force, the whole society will be in chaos.

I am not in favor of chaos. I want human society to become a harmonious whole, a vast commune all around the world: People meditating, people without guilt, people with great serenity, silence; people rejoicing, dancing, singing; people who have no desire to compete with anyone; people who have dropped the very idea that they are special and have to prove it by becoming the president of America; people who are no longer suffering from any inferiority complex, so nobody wants to be superior, nobody brags about his greatness.

> If you are sick, medicines are needed. An anarchist like Kropotkin wants to destroy the medicines. I want you to be healthy so you don't need medicines. Automatically you will throw them out—what will you do with all those medicines?

Governments will evaporate like dewdrops in the early morning sun. But that is a totally different story, a totally different approach. Till that moment comes, governments are needed.

It is a simple thing. If you are sick, medicines are needed. An anarchist like Kropotkin wants to destroy the medicines. I want you to be healthy so you don't need medicines. Automatically you will throw them out. What will you do with all those medicines? They are utterly useless, in fact, dangerous; most medicines are poisons. For what purpose will you go on accumulating them? See the difference of emphasis.

I am not against medicines; I am against the sickness of human beings which makes medicines necessary. I would like a healthier human being—which is possible with genetic engineering—a human being who has no possibility of becoming sick because we have programmed him from his very birth in such a way that he cannot be sick, we have made arrangements in his body to fight against any sickness. Certainly medicines would disappear, pharmacies would disappear, doctors would disappear, medical colleges would be closed. But not because I am against them! That will be simply a consequence of a healthy humanity.

I want one world, one language, one religiousness, one humanity—and when humanity is really grown-up in consciousness, one government.

Government is not something to brag about. It is an insult. Its existence says to you that you are still barbarous, civilization has not happened; otherwise why do you need a government to rule you?

If all crime disappears, if all the fears that others can exploit you, murder you, disappear, what will you do with this whole bureaucracy of government? You cannot continue it, because it is a burden on the economy of the nation, a big burden, and it goes on becoming bigger and bigger. The hierarchies have a tendency to become bigger and bigger for the simple reason that everybody wants not to work, everybody hates work. So everybody needs more assistance; the work is growing.

In any government office, you can see files just piled up on the tables. Unless you are able to bribe someone, your file may remain somewhere in the huge pile; it will never come to the top. And the bureaucrats enjoy having many files there; it makes them important, special. They have power over so many people; in their minds, all these files contain their power over people.

I am an anarchist of a totally different category from those who have existed before on the earth. I am a category in myself, because my approach is radically different. I am not against government, I am against the need for government. I am not against the courts, I am against the need for the courts.

Someday, some time, I see the possibility that man will be able to live without any control—religious or political—because he will be a discipline unto himself.

There is a story of a disciple who comes to see his master and asks him whether man is free.

The master tells his disciple to stand up and to lift one of his feet off the ground. The disciple, standing on one leg—and the other one in the air—understands less than before. Now the master asks him to also lift the other foot off the ground.

Osho, can you speak on the difference between freedom for and freedom from?

Freedom from is ordinary, mundane. Man has always tried to be free from things. It is not creative. It is the negative aspect of freedom. Freedom for is creativity. You have a certain vision that you would like to materialize and you want freedom for it.

Freedom from is always from the past, and freedom for is always for the future.

Freedom for is a spiritual dimension because you are moving into the unknown and perhaps, one day, into the unknowable. It will give you wings. Freedom from, at the most, can take away your handcuffs. It is not necessarily beneficial—and the whole of history is proof of it. People have never thought of the second freedom that I am insisting on; they have only thought of the first—because they don't have the insight to see the second. The first is visible: chains on their feet, handcuffs on their hands. They want to be free from them, but then what? What are you going to do with your hands? You may even repent that you asked for freedom from.

It happened in the castle of the Bastille during the French Revolution. It was the most famous French prison; it was reserved only for those who were sentenced to life imprisonment. So one entered the Bastille alive but never came out alive—only the dead bodies came out. And when they put on the handcuffs, the chains, they locked them and threw the keys in a well which was inside the Bastille—because they were not needed. Those locks would not be opened again, so what would be their use? There were more than five thousand people in that prison. What is the use of keeping five thousand peoples' keys and maintaining them unnecessarily? Once they have entered their dark cells, they have entered them forever.

The French revolutionaries of course thought that the first thing that had to be done was to free the people from the Bastille. It is inhuman to put somebody for any act whatsoever into prison in a dark cell just to wait for his death, which might come fifty years afterwards, sixty years afterwards. Sixty years of waiting is an immense torture to the soul. It is not punishment, it is vengeance, revenge because these people disobeyed the law. There is no balance between their acts and the punishment.

The revolutionaries opened the doors, they dragged people out from their dark cells. And they were surprised. Those people were not ready to leave their cells.

You can understand. A person who has lived for sixty years in darkness—the sun is too much for him. He does not want to come out into the light. His eyes have become too delicate. And what is the point? He is now eighty years old. When he entered he was twenty. His whole life has been in this darkness. This darkness has become his home.

And the revolutionaries wanted to make the prisoners free. They broke their chains, their handcuffs—because there were no keys. But the prisoners were very resistant. They did not want to leave the prison. They said, "You don't understand our condition. A man who has been sixty years in this position, what will he do outside? Who will provide him food? Here food is given, and he can rest in his peaceful, dark cell. He knows he is almost dead. Outside he will not be able to find his wife or know what has happened to her; his parents will have died; his friends will have died or may have completely forgotten him. And nobody is going to give him a job. A man who has been for sixty years out of work, who is going to give him a job?—and a man from the Bastille, where the most dangerous criminals were kept? Just the name Bastille will be enough to have him denied any job. Why are you forcing us? Where will we sleep? We don't have any houses. We have almost forgotten where we used to live—somebody else must be living there. Our houses, our families, our friends, our whole world has changed so much in sixty years; we will not be able to make it. Don't torture us more. We have been tortured enough."

And there was reasonableness in what they were saying. But revolutionaries are stubborn people; they wouldn't listen. They forced the men out of the Bastille, but by that night almost everybody had come back. They said, "Give us food because we are hungry."

A few came in the middle of the night and they said, "Give us our chains back because we cannot sleep without them. We have slept for fifty, sixty years with handcuffs, with chains on our legs, in darkness. They have become almost part of our bodies, we cannot sleep without them. You return our chains—and we want our cells. We were perfectly happy. Don't force your revolution on us. We are poor people. You can do your revolution somewhere else."

The revolutionaries were shocked. But the incident shows that freedom *from* is not necessarily a blessing.

You can see it all around the world; countries have become free from the British Empire, from the Spanish Empire, from the Portuguese Empire—but their situation is far worse than it was when they were slaves. At least in their slavery they had become accustomed to it. They had dropped ambitions, they had accepted their situation as their destiny.

<u>Freedom from slavery simply creates chaos.</u>

My whole family was involved in India's freedom struggle. They had all been to jail. Their education was disturbed. None could graduate from the university because before they could pass the examination they were caught—one was three years in jail, one was four years in jail. And then it was too late to start again, and they had become bona fide revolutionaries. In jail they contacted all the leaders of revolution; then their whole lives were devoted to revolution.

I was small but I used to argue with my father, with my uncles: "I can understand that slavery is ugly, it dehumanizes you, humiliates you, it degrades you from the prestige of being a human being; it should be fought against. But my point is, what will you do when you are free? Freedom *from* is clear, and I am not against it. What I want to know and understand clearly is <u>what you are going to do with your freedom</u>. You know how to live in slavery. Do you know how to live in freedom? You know a certain order has to be maintained in slavery; otherwise you will be crushed, killed, shot. Do you know that in freedom it will be your responsibility to maintain the order? Nobody will be killing you and nobody else will be responsible for it—you have to be responsible for it. Have you asked your leaders what this freedom is for?"

And I never received any answer. They said, "Right now we are so involved in getting rid of slavery; we will take care of freedom later on."

I said, "This is not a scientific attitude. If you are demolishing the old house, if you are intelligent you should at least prepare a blueprint for the new house. It would be best if you prepare the new house before you demolish the old. Otherwise you will be without a house and then you will suffer—because it is better to be in the old house than to be without a house."

In my family, great leaders of the Indian revolution used to stay with us—and this was my constant argument with them. And I never found a single leader of the revolution who had the answer to what they were going to do with freedom.

Freedom came. Hindus and Mohammedans killed each other in millions. They had been kept from killing each other by the British forces; the forces were removed and there were riots all over India. Everybody's life was in danger. Whole towns were burning; whole trains were burning, and people were not allowed to get out of the burning trains.

I said, "This is strange. It was not happening in slavery, but it is happening in freedom—and the reason simply is that you were not prepared for what freedom is."

The country was divided into two parts—they had never thought about it. In the whole country there was chaos, and the people who came to power had a certain expertise—that expertise was in burning the bridges and the jails, in killing the people who were enslaving the country. This expertise had nothing to do with building a new country. But these were the leaders of the revolution; naturally they came to power. They had fought, they had won, and the power came into their hands. And it was the wrong hands.

No revolutionary should be given power—because he knows how to sabotage but he does not know how to create; he only knows how to destroy. He should be honored, respected, given gold medals and everything, but don't give him power.

You will have to find people who can be creative—but these will be the people who have not participated in revolution.

This is a very delicate matter. Because the creative people were concerned with their creativity, they were not interested in who rules. Somebody must rule, but whether it is the British or the Indians doesn't matter to them. They were concerned with pouring their energy into their creative work, so they were not in the revolutionary ranks. Now, the revolutionaries will not allow them to have power. In fact, they are the renegades. These are the people who never participated in revolution, and you are giving power to them?

So every revolution has failed in the world up to now, and for the simple reason that the people who make the revolution have one kind of expertise and the people who can make a country, create a country, create responsibility in people, are a different group. They don't participate in destruction, murder. But they cannot get into power. Power goes into the hands of those who have been fighting. So, naturally, every revolution is intrinsically bound to fail unless what I am saying is understood clearly.

There are two parts to revolution, from and for; and there should be two kinds of revolutionaries: those who are working for the first—that is freedom from—and those who will work when the work of the first is finished, for freedom for. But it is difficult to manage. Who will manage it? Everybody is full of lust for power. When the revolutionaries are victorious, the power is theirs; they cannot give it to anybody else and the country falls into chaos. And every day in every dimension it will get worse.

> No revolutionary should be given the power—because he knows how to sabotage but he does not know how to create, he only knows how to destroy. He should be honored, respected, given gold medals and everything, but don't give him power.

That is why I don't teach revolution; I teach you rebellion. Revolution is of the crowd; rebellion is of the individual. The individual changes himself. He does not care about the power structure; he simply manages to change his own being, gives birth to a new man in himself. And if the whole country is rebellious . . .

The most wonderful thing about it is this: in rebellion, both kinds of revolutionaries can participate, because in rebellion much has to be destroyed and much has to be created. Things have to be destroyed in order to create, so it has an appeal for all—for those who are interested in destruction and those who are interested in creativity.

It is not a crowd phenomenon. It is your own individuality. And if millions of people go through rebellion, then the power of countries, nations is going to be in the hands of these people—who are rebels. Only in rebellion can revolution succeed; otherwise, revolution has a split personality.

Rebellion is one, single.

And remember this: in rebellion, destructiveness and creativity go hand in hand, supporting each other. They are not separate processes. Once you make them separate—as they are in revolution—you will repeat the story.

The story in the question is not complete. It is a beautiful, mystic story.

A man comes to a master to ask how much man is independent, free. Is he totally free, or is there a limitation? Is there something like fate, kismet, destiny, a God who makes a limitation beyond which you cannot be free?

The mystic answered in his own way—not logically but existentially. He said, "Stand up."

The man must have felt this was a stupid kind of answer, "I am asking a simple question and he is asking me to stand up." But he said, "Let us see what happens." He stood.

And the mystic said, "Now, raise one of your legs up."

The man, by this time, must have been thinking he had come to a madman; what has this to do with freedom, independence? But now that he has come . . . and there must have been a crowd of disciples, and the mystic was so respected; not to follow him would be disrespectful, and there was no harm. So he lifted one of his legs from the earth, so one foot was in the air and he was standing on one foot.

And then the master said, "That's perfectly good. Just one thing more. Now take the other foot up also."

That is impossible! The man said, "You are asking something impossible. I have taken my right foot up. Now I cannot take my left foot up."

The master said, "But you were free. In the beginning you could have taken the left foot up. There was no binding order. You were completely free to choose whether to take the left foot up or the right foot up. I had not said anything about it, you decided. You took the right foot up. In your very decision you made it impossible for the left foot to be lifted up. Don't bother about fate, kismet, God. Just think of simple things."

Any act that you do prevents you from doing some other act that goes against it. So every act is a limitation. In the story it is so clear. In life it is not so clear because you can't see one foot on the earth and one foot in the air. But each act, each decision is a limitation.

You are totally free before deciding, but once you have decided, your very decision, your very choice brings in a limitation. Nobody else is imposing the decision; it is the nature of things— you cannot do contradictory things together simultaneously. And it is good you cannot; otherwise, you are already in chaos, you would be in greater chaos if you were allowed to do contradictory things together. You would go mad. This is simply an existential safety measure.

Basically you are totally free to choose, but once you choose, your very choice brings a limitation.

If you want to remain totally free, then don't choose. That's where the teaching of choiceless awareness comes in. Why the insistence of the great masters just to be aware and not to choose? Because the moment you choose, you have lost your total freedom, you are left with only a part. But if you remain choiceless, your freedom remains total.

There is only one thing which is totally free and that is choiceless awareness. Everything else is limited.

You love a woman—she is beautiful but very poor. You love riches—there is another woman who is very rich but ugly, disgusting. Now you have to choose. And whatever you choose, you will suffer. If you choose the beautiful girl who is poor, you will always repent that you missed all those riches unnecessarily—because the beauty after a few days' acquaintance is taken for granted, you don't see it. And what will you do with beauty? You cannot purchase a car, you cannot purchase a house, you cannot purchase anything. Now beat your head with your beauty—what you will do? So the mind starts thinking that the choice was wrong.

> Basically you are totally free to choose, but once you choose, your very choice brings a limitation. If you want to remain totally free, then don't choose.

But if you choose the disgusting, ugly woman, you would have all that money can purchase: a palace, servants, all the gadgets, but you will have to tolerate that woman—not only tolerate but to say

"I love you." And you cannot even hate her, she is so disgusting. Even to hate, one needs somebody who is not disgusting because hate is a relationship. And you cannot enjoy those cars and the palace and the garden, because the disgusting face of that woman will be constantly following you. And she knows that you have not married her, you have married her riches, so she is going to treat you like a servant, not like a lover. And it is the truth: you have not loved her. Then you will start thinking it would have been better to have a poor house, ordinary food—at least the woman was beautiful, you would have enjoyed her. You have been an idiot to choose this.

Whatever you choose you will repent because the other will remain and haunt you.

If one needs absolute freedom, then choiceless awareness is the only answer.

And when I say instead of revolution go for rebellion, I am bringing you closer to a complete whole. In revolution you are bound to be divided, either *from* something or *for* something. You cannot have both together because they need different expertise. But in rebellion both qualities are combined together.

When a sculptor makes a statue he is doing both; he is cutting the stone—destroying the stone as it was—and he is, by destroying the stone, creating a beautiful statue that was not there before. Destruction and creation go together; they are not divided.

Rebellion is whole.

Revolution is half and half—and that is the danger of revolution. The word is beautiful, but down through the centuries it has become associated with a split mind. And I am against all kinds of splits because they will make you schizophrenic.

Now all the countries that have been freed from slavery are going through an inconceivable agony. It was not like that when they were slaves, and they had been slaves for three or four hundred years. In those years, they never encountered such agony; but in just a few decades they have gone through such hell that they wonder, "Why were we fighting for freedom? If this is freedom, then slavery was far better." Slavery is never better. It is just that these people don't realize that they have chosen only half freedom.

The other half can be achieved, but not by the same people who brought about the revolution. The other half will need a totally different kind of intelligence and wisdom. And the revolutionaries who murder and throw bombs and burn trains and police stations and post offices—those are not the people who are needed now.

In my family, only my grandfather was against sending my uncles to universities. It was my father who somehow managed to send them there. My grandfather said, "You don't know. I understand these boys. You will be sending them to the university and they will end up in jail—such is the atmosphere."

Most of the revolution was led by students, young people. Knowing nothing of life—they had not experienced anything—but they had energy, they had vitality; they were young and had this romantic idea of being free. They did everything—making and throwing bombs and killing bureaucrats and politicians. They did it all. And when they were released from jail, they suddenly found they had all the power but they did not have the skill to use it. They had no intelligence either—what to do with it? They pretended. They enjoyed the euphoria, and the country also enjoyed it for the moment—now our own people are in power!—but soon they started fighting with each other.

Revolution has the problem—and I think it always will—that it is undertaken by one kind of people and all power will come into their hands. The lust for power is just human. The revolutionaries will not want to give this power to anybody else, but that is exactly what has to be done. New people have to be found who are wise enough—creative, intelligent—who can help the country in all possible ways by bringing in new technology, new methods of agriculture; who can introduce new industries in the country; who can open the country's doors to world investment.

But just the opposite happened in India. The country started falling apart every day; it began to deteriorate. And it went on deteriorating and nobody would point out the simple fact that the wrong people were in power.

Just give the revolutionaries honor, give them prizes, give them awards, great certificates written in golden letters that they can put in their houses—but don't give them power.

Seeing the disastrous situation of all revolutions, I started thinking about rebellion—which is individual. And the individual can be capable of synthesizing the destructive and the creative forces together in his choiceless awareness.

And if many people go through this rebellion—which is not against anybody, but is just against your own conditioning—and bring forth a new human being within themselves, then the problem is not difficult to solve.

Revolution should become outdated.

If you fight and struggle, do you think you will able to transform the world and its situation? You will become like those people against whom you are fighting and struggling; that is one of the fundamental laws of life. Choose your enemies very carefully! Friends you can choose without care. There is no need to be worried about friends because they don't have the same impact on you as does the enemy. You have to be very careful with the enemy because you will have to fight the enemy. In fighting, you will have to use the same strategies, the same tactics. And you will have to use those strategies and tactics for years and years; they will condition you. That is how it has happened down through the ages.

Joseph Stalin proved a far more dangerous czar than the czars who had ruled Russia before communism took over. Why? Because Stalin had learned the strategy from the czars. Fighting with the czars, he learned the same tactics that they were using. His whole life was spent in fighting, practicing violence, by the time he came to power Stalin was a czar, far more dangerous, obviously, because he had succeeded against the czars. He must have been more cunning, more violent, more ambitious, and more Machiavellian. Otherwise it would have been impossible for him to win against the czars.

And he did it on a far greater scale: he defeated all the czars! All the czars put together had never committed as much violence and murder as Joseph Stalin alone did. Stalin had learned the lesson so well that it is suspected that the leader of the revolution, Lenin, was poisoned by him. Lenin was ill, and in the name of medicine he was poisoned slowly and was killed by the poison. If Lenin had survived, then Joseph Stalin would have become the number three man, because there was another man, Leon Trotsky, who was number two. So Stalin's first priority was to destroy Lenin—he killed Lenin—and then the second was to kill Trotsky, which he did. Then Stalin was in power, and once he was in power he started killing everybody—all the members of the Politburo, and by and by the highest ranking communist leaders. Because they all knew the strategies, they had to be removed.

> This world is a very beautiful world but it is in the wrong hands—but when I say that, I don't mean that you start fighting with those wrong hands. What I mean is please don't *you* be those wrong hands, that's all.

This has happened in all the revolutions in the world.

This world is a very beautiful world but it is in the wrong

hands—but when I say that, I don't mean that you start fighting with those wrong hands. What I mean is, please, don't *you* be those wrong hands, that's all.

I don't teach revolution, I teach rebellion, and the difference is great. Revolution is political; rebellion is religious. Revolution needs you to organize yourself as a party, as an army, and fight against the enemies. Rebellion means you rebel as an individual; you simply get out of this whole rut. At least you should not destroy nature.

And if more and more people become dropouts, the world can be saved. That will be true revolution, nonpolitical; it will be spiritual. If more and more people get out of the old mind and its ways, if more and more people become loving, nonambitious, nongreedy, if more and more people are no longer interested in power politics, in prestige, and respectability. . . . If more and more people start dropping out of the old, rotten game and living life on their own. . . . It is not a struggle against the old, it is simply getting out of the clutches of the old—and this is the only way to weaken it; this is the only way to destroy it.

If millions of people simply get out of the hands of the politicians, the politicians will die of their own accord. You cannot fight with them. If you fight you become a politician yourself. If you struggle against them, you become greedy and ambitious yourself, and that is not going to help.

Be a dropout. And you have a small life: for the fifty, sixty, seventy years more you may be here, you can't hope that you will be able to transform the world, but you can hope that you can still enjoy and love the world.

Use the opportunity of this life to celebrate as much as possible. Don't waste it in struggling and fighting.

I am trying to create a political force; no, not at all. All political revolutions have failed so utterly that only blind people can go on believing in them. Those who have eyes are bound to teach you something new. This is something new. It has been done before too, but not on a large scale. We have to do it now on a large scale—millions of people have to become dropouts! By dropouts I don't mean that you leave society and go live in the mountains. You continue to live in society but you leave the ambition, the greed, and the hatred. Live in the society and be loving, and live as a nobody; then you can enjoy and you can celebrate. And by celebrating and enjoying, you will spread the ripples of ecstasy to other people.

We can change the whole world, but not by struggle—not this time. Enough is enough! We have to change this world by celebrating, by dancing, by singing, by music, by meditation, by love. Not by struggle.

The old certainly has to cease for the new to be, but please don't misinterpret me. Certainly the old has to cease—but the old is within you, not without. I am not talking about the old structure of society; I am talking about the old structure of your mind that has to cease in order for the new to be. And a single person dropping the old structure of the

> Certainly the old has to cease—but the old is within you, not without. I am not talking about the old structure of the society, I am talking about the old structure of your mind that has to cease in order for the new to be.

mind creates such a great space for many to transform their lives that it is incredible, unimaginable, unbelievable. A single person transforming himself becomes a trigger; then many more start changing. His presence becomes a catalytic agent.

This is the rebellion I teach: you drop out of the old structure, you drop out of the old greed, you drop out of the old idealism.

You become a silent, meditative, loving person. Be more in a dance, and then see what happens. Somebody, sooner or later, is bound to join the dance with you, and then more and more people will.

I have no political leanings. I am utterly against politics. Yes, the old has to cease for the new to be—but the old has to cease *within you*, then the new will be there. And once the new is within you the new is infectious, contagious; it starts spreading into other people.

Joy is contagious! Laugh, and you will see that others start laughing. So is it with sadness: be sad, and somebody looking at your long face suddenly becomes sad. We are not separate, we are joined together, so when somebody's heart starts laughing many other hearts are touched—sometimes even faraway hearts. You have come from such faraway places; somehow my laughter has reached you, my love has reached you. Somehow, in some mysterious way, my being has touched your being and you have come here against all the difficulties.

But I am not teaching you to struggle against anything. Whenever you struggle against anything you become a reactionary—because this *is* a reaction. You become obsessed with something, you are against it, and then there is every possibility that the thing you are against will dominate you—maybe in a negative way, but it will dominate you.

Friedrich Nietzsche was very much opposed to Jesus Christ. But my own analysis of Friedrich Nietzsche is that he was too much impressed by Jesus Christ, just because he was against him. He was obsessed; he was really trying to become a Jesus Christ in his own right. His great book, *Thus Spake Zarathustra*, is an effort to create a new gospel. The language he uses, the metaphors, the poetry certainly reminds one of Jesus Christ, and Nietzsche was very much against him. He never missed a single opportunity—if he could condemn Jesus, he would immediately condemn him. But one is reminded again and again of Jesus. He was obsessed. When he became mad, in the last phase of his life, he even started signing his letters as "Anti-Christ Friedrich Nietzsche." He could not forget Christ even when he became mad. First he would write "Anti-Christ" and then he would sign his name. You can see the obsession, the deep jealousy of Jesus that dominated him his whole life. It destroyed his immense creativity. He could have been a rebel but he reduced himself to a reactionary. He might have brought something new to the world, but he could not. He remained obsessed with Jesus.

I am not against anything or anybody. I don't want you to be free *from* something, I simply want you to be free. See the difference: freedom *from* is never total; that "from" keeps it entrapped with the past. Freedom *from* can never be real freedom.

OBSTACLES AND STEPPING-STONES: RESPONSES TO QUESTIONS

There are many kinds of freedom—social, political, economic—but they are only superficial. True freedom has a totally different dimension to it. It is not concerned with the outside world at all; it arises within you. It is freedom from all kinds of conditioning, religious ideologies, political philosophies.

All that has been imposed on you by others fetters you, chains you, imprisons you, makes you spiritually a slave.

Meditation is nothing but the destruction of all these fetters and conditionings, the destruction of the whole prison so that you can again be free under the sky and the stars, out in the open, available to existence.

The moment you are available to existence, existence is available to you. And the meeting of those two availabilities is ultimate bliss. But it can happen only in freedom. Freedom is the highest value; there is nothing higher.

On the one hand you are suggesting we should have ultimate free-
dom to do whatever we want to do, and on the other hand you are
saying we have to take responsibility. With responsibility, I cannot
use the word "freedom" as I want. When I understand what you are
saying, I feel grateful. But mostly I see that I would rather think of
freedom as license.

It is one of the perennial questions of humanity: the question of freedom and responsibility. If you are free, you interpret it to mean that now there is no responsibility. Just a hundred years ago Friedrich Nietzsche declared, "God is dead, and man is free." And the next sentence he wrote is, "Now you can do whatsoever you want to do. There is no responsibility. God is dead, man is free, and there is no responsibility." There he was absolutely wrong; when there is no God, there is tremendous responsibility on your shoulders. If there is a God, he can share your responsibility. You can throw your responsibility on Him: you can say, "It is you who have made the world; it is you who have made me in this way; it is you who is finally, ultimately, responsible, not me. How can I be ultimately responsible? I am just a creature, and you are the creator. Why have you put seeds of corruption and seeds of sin in me from the beginning? You are responsible. I am free." In fact, if there is no God, then man is absolutely responsible for his acts, because there is no way to unload that responsibility on anyone else.

When I say to you that you are free, I mean that you are responsible. You cannot throw responsibility on anybody else; you are alone. And whatever you do is your responsibility. You cannot say that somebody else forced you to do it because you are free; nobody can force you! Because you are free, it is your decision to do something or not. With freedom comes responsibility. Freedom is responsibility. But the mind is very cunning, the mind interprets in its own way: it always listens to what it wants to listen to. It goes on

interpreting things in its own way. The mind never tries to understand what is really the truth. It has made that decision already.

I have heard:

"I am a respectable man, doctor, but lately life has become
intolerable because of my feelings of guilt and self-
recrimination." The patient gulped miserably before continuing. "You see, I have recently fallen victim to an
uncontrollable urge to pinch and fondle girls in the underground."

"Dearie me," tutted the psychiatrist consolingly, "we
must certainly help you to rid yourself of this unfortunate
urge. I can quite see how distressing . . ."

The patient broke in anxiously, "It is not so much the
urge I wanted to get rid of for me, doctor, it is the guilt."

People go on talking about freedom, but they don't want freedom exactly; they want irresponsibility. They ask for freedom, but
deep down, unconsciously, they ask for irresponsibility, license.

Freedom is maturity; license is childish. Freedom is possible
only when you are so integrated that you can accept the responsibility of being free. The world is not free because people are not
mature. Revolutionaries have tried many things down through the
centuries, but it all fails. Utopians always contemplate about how to
make man free, but nobody bothers—because man cannot be free
unless he is integrated. Only a Buddha can be free, a Mahavira, a
Christ, a Mohammed can be free, a Zarathustra can be free, because
freedom means man is now aware. If you are not aware, then you
need the state, the government, the police, and the courts. Then
freedom has to be curtailed. Then freedom exists in name only; in
fact, it doesn't exist at all. How can freedom exist when governments exist? It is impossible. But what to do about it?

If governments disappear, there will be anarchy, not freedom. It will be a worse state than it is now. It will be sheer madness. Police are needed because you are not alert. Otherwise, what is the point of having a policeman standing at a crossroad? If people are alert, the policeman can be removed, because he will become unnecessary. But people are not conscious, the policeman is needed.

So when I say "freedom," I mean be responsible. The more responsible you become, the more free you become; or, the more free you become, the more you take responsibility. Then you have to be very alert about what you are doing and what you are saying. You have to be conscious about even your smallest gestures because there is nobody else to control you. When I say to you that you are free, I mean that you are a god. Freedom is not license; it is a tremendous discipline.

> Freedom is possible only when you are so integrated that you can take the responsibility of being free. The world is not free because people are not mature.

For forty-five years I lived in prison, mostly made by myself. Now I know it is possible to become more and more free. But what to do when you feel the need for a safe place, a good climate to grow? Another prison? How to be free anywhere, any time? I feel sorrow and rebellion in me about that.

Freedom has nothing to do with the outside; one can be free even in an actual prison. Freedom is something inner; it is of the consciousness. You can be free anywhere—chained, in a jail, you can be free—and you can be unfree outside the jail, in your own home; visibly free, but you will be a prisoner if your consciousness is not free.

You are confusing outer freedom with inner freedom. As far as the outside is concerned, you can never be absolutely free—let that be clear once and for all. As far as outside is concerned, you are not alone, so how can you be absolutely free? There are millions of people around you. On the outside, life has to be a compromise. If you were alone on the earth, you would have been absolutely free; but you are not alone.

On the road you have to keep to the left. And the questioner will feel this is a great bondage: "Why? Why should I be forced to be on the left? I am a free woman. If I want to walk on the right, I will walk on the right. If I want to walk in the middle of the road, I will walk in the middle of the road." In India you can do it—India is a free country, remember! It is the greatest democracy in the world, so right, left, middle, you can walk anywhere!

But one individual's freedom becomes so many people's problem. You are free to be yourself, but you should not interfere in other people's lives.

A man of understanding will respect his freedom as much as he will respect others' freedom, because if nobody respects your freedom, your freedom will be destroyed. It is dependent on a mutual understanding: "I respect your freedom, you respect my freedom, then we both can be free." But it is a compromise. I will not interfere with your being and I will not trespass on you.

For example, you want to sing loudly in the middle of the night. Of course you are a free person, and if you cannot sing loudly in your own house, what kind of freedom is this? But the neighbors have to sleep too; so there has to be a compromise.

On the outside we are interdependent. Nobody can be absolutely independent. Life is interdependence. Not only are you interdependent with people, you are interdependent with everything. If you cut down all the trees, you will die because they constantly supply you with oxygen. You are dependent on them—and they are dependent on you. We take in oxygen and exhale carbon dioxide; the trees do just the opposite, they exhale oxygen and inhale carbon dioxide.

So when people are smoking, the trees must be very happy because more carbon dioxide is being created for them! These trees will be very sad when I tell you to go to the root cause of it and then smoking will disappear. That means trees won't get as much carbon dioxide as they got before!

We are interdependent not only with the trees but also with the sun, the moon, and the stars. Everything is an interdependence. Enjoy this interdependence. Don't call it bondage. It is not dependence, it is *inter*dependence. You are dependent on others; others are dependent on you. It is a brotherhood; it is relatedness. Even the smallest grass leaf is related to the greatest star.

But in the inner world, in the inner kingdom, you can be absolutely free. And then you will not

> On the outside, life has to be a compromise. If you were alone on the earth you would have been absolutely free, but you are not alone.

feel sad and rebellious; there is no need. Understand that the outer interdependence is a must, it is inevitable; nothing can be done about it. It is part of how things are. Accept it. When nothing can be done about it, acceptance is the only way. And accept it joyously, not in resignation. Accept it! This is our universe; we are part of it. We are not islands; we are part of the whole continent. We are not egos.

Your idea of freedom is rooted somewhere in the idea of the ego. We are not egos. The ego is a false entity. Because we are not separate, how can we have egos? As far as language is concerned, it is utilitarian to use the word "I," but it has no substance to it. It is pure shadow, utterly empty. A useful word, utilitarian, but not real.

But inner freedom *is* possible. It happens as you go deeper and deeper into awareness. Watch your body; watch your thought processes. Watch, and witness the whole process of your thoughts. And slowly you will see you are neither anger nor greed, neither Hindu nor Mohammedan nor Christian, neither Catholic nor communist. Slowly you will become aware that you are not any thought—you are not the mind at all. You are a pure witness. The experience of pure witnessing is the experience of total freedom, but it is an inward phenomenon. And a person who is inwardly totally free has no hankering to be outwardly free. Such a person is capable of accepting nature as it is.

> A person who is inwardly totally free has no hankering to be outwardly free. Such a person is capable of accepting nature as it is.

Create inner freedom through witnessing, and live out of inner freedom and then you will be able to see the interdependence on the outside. It is beautiful and it is a blessing. There is no need to rebel against it. Relax into it, surrender to it. And remember: only a person who is really free can surrender.

Doesn't the word "rebel" imply fighting against something? The word itself comes from the Latin rebellare, *fighting back. When you speak about the rebel, you speak of it in a positive sense. Are you changing the meaning of the word?*

I am not changing the meaning of the word; I am making it complete. The meaning that has been given to it is only half . . . just the negative meaning; and no negative can exist without a positive. It is true, the word "rebel" comes from the Latin *rebellare*, fighting back. But that is only half of the meaning; the other half has been missing for centuries, from the very beginning. Nobody has bothered to complete the whole meaning of the word. Fighting against is only the beginning. But fighting for what?

And it is not only true of the word "rebel," it is true of many words. "Freedom" has only a negative connotation in people's minds—freedom from. But nobody asks about freedom for. Freedom from is an essential part, but only the negative part. Unless you have a positive goal, your freedom from is meaningless. You should also be clearly aware of what you are fighting for: What is the goal of your freedom?

"Rebel" and "rebellion" have been condemned, and this is part of the condemnation—that they have been given only the negative meaning in the dictionaries by the linguists. Nobody has raised the question, "Rebellion for what?" should be the essential question. To me, the negative part is only the beginning, not the end. The positive part is the end, and it completes the whole circle.

You rebel against what is dead, and you rebel for what is living. You rebel against superstitions, and you rebel for truth. Otherwise, what is the need to rebel against superstitions? Any rebellion is incomplete and futile if it is only negative. Only the positive will make it meaningful and significant.

Remember this about all words—if society has kept only the negative meaning, that means it is against those words. Not only is it against actual rebellion, it is even against the word "rebellion"; it has given it a negative color. To give it a positive color, a positive beauty, will mean support for it.

I am not changing the meaning of rebellion, I am simply completing it; it has been incomplete for too long. It needs completion and the last finishing touches, so that it can regain the beauty that has been taken away from it.

Society has been very cunning about all aspects of life—it has manipulated words, language, and everything so that it supports the establishment. Even language needs to be freed from the chains that have bound it in the past. Beautiful words like "rebel," "revolution," and "freedom" have to be redeemed from negativity. And the only way to do this is to make the center of the world positive;

> ❧
>
> Unless you have a positive goal, your freedom from is meaningless. You should also be clearly aware of what you are fighting for: What is the goal of your freedom?

the negative is only preparation for the positive. When you prepare the ground for a garden, you take away the weeds, the unnecessary growth of wild plants, and their roots—the negative part.

But just taking away the weeds, the wild plants and their roots, and cleaning the ground is not enough to make a garden. It is necessary, but not enough. You will have to plant roses also; that will be the positive part. You will have to plant beautiful flowers, beautiful trees. The negative part is only a preparation for something positive to happen.

I've come to feel a tremendous sense of freedom over the years in the sense that I no longer feel imprisoned by nationality or place, or my own personal history. But there is also a sense of sadness mixed with this freedom. What is this sadness?

Freedom has two sides, and if you experience only one side of it, a single side, you will feel freedom mixed with sadness. You have to understand the whole psychology of freedom.

The first side is freedom *from*: from nationality, from a certain church, a certain race, a certain political ideology. This is the first part of freedom, the foundation of freedom. It is always *from* something. Once you have attained this freedom, you will feel very light and good and happy. And for the first time you will start rejoicing in your own individuality, because your individuality was covered with all those things that you have become free of.

But this is only one half—and then the sadness will come, because the other half is missing. Freedom *from* is fulfilled, but freedom for what? Freedom in itself has no meaning, unless it is freedom *for* something, something creative—freedom to sculpt, freedom to dance, freedom to create music, poetry, painting. Unless your freedom turns into a creative realization, you will feel sad. Because you will see that you are free—your chains are broken, and you are no longer in prison; you are standing under the starry night, completely free. But where do you go?

Then comes a sudden sadness. What path do you choose? Up to now there was no question of going anywhere—you were imprisoned. Your whole consciousness was concentrated on how to get free, and that was your only anxiety. Now that you are free, a new kind of problem has to be encountered. What to do now that you are free?

Freedom itself does not mean anything unless you choose a creative path. Either you go deeper into meditation for self-realization, or, if you have a certain kind of talent that has not been allowed to develop because of your fetters—you could not compose music because your hands were in chains, you could not dance because your feet were in chains. If you have a talent to be a dancer, then be a dancer—then your freedom is complete the circle is complete.

Freedom *from* and freedom *for*—it is a dilemma that is being faced by every person who struggles first for freedom and then suddenly finds, "Now that I am free, what am I going to do?" Up till now, he was totally occupied and so busy, even in his dreams he was thinking only of freedom. And he never thought about what he was going to do when he got it.

But something more is needed. You have to become a creator. You have to find some creativity that fulfills your freedom; otherwise the freedom is empty. You need either to create something or discover something, either bring your potential to actuality or go inwards to find yourself, but you need to do something with your freedom. Freedom only provides an opportunity for you; it is not the goal itself. It simply gives you the opportunity to do whatever you want to do. When you are free and are feeling sad, it is because you have not used this opportunity yet.

Meditation will do, music will do, sculpture, dancing, or love. But do something with your freedom; don't just idly by or you will become sad.

Freedom has to be a creative force in your life, not just a negative one. Now that you are no longer imprisoned, you find yourself standing free beneath the sky, but completely lost. Perhaps you never realized before now that the imprisoned person has a reason for remaining imprisoned. That's why millions of people in the world remain prisoners of religion, caste, creed, nation, color. They go on tolerating their prisons because when they are imprisoned they don't have any responsibility; they don't have to be creators; they don't have to find some positivity in their freedom. It is enough for them to remain imprisoned because others will go on taking care of everything.

Why are people Christians, Hindus, or Mohammedans? Because Jesus will take care of you. You need not be worried. You just have to be a slave of the Christian church, and the church will take care of your sins and all else that is needed. You feel absolutely unburdened; you have no responsibility.

But remember one thing fundamental to the whole question of freedom: responsibility and freedom go together. If you don't want to have responsibility, you can't have freedom either. They come together or they go together. If you give up responsibility, you have to accept slavery in some way or another.

Up till now, you had dreamed about freedom without thinking about the great responsibility that will follow. You now have freedom, but you have not fulfilled the responsibility yet. Hence, a sadness lingers around you. You are capable of destroying this sadness. If you were capable of coming out of your slavery, you are certainly capable of being creative. If you were able to destroy your prisons, you can certainly create something beautiful.

My own experience is that unless you become a creator in some way, your life will remain empty and sad. The only blissful people are the creators. It may be simply the creation of more consciousness, more experience of truth, consciousness, bliss. It may be an inner world of creativity or it may be something outer. But freedom has to become responsible, positive. Your freedom is still negative. It is good that you are out of prison, but it is not enough. Now you have to earn your bread. Up to now, the jailers were supplying the bread. Along with the chains, they were supplying you with shelter and clothes.

So many people belong to churches, synagogues, or temples. Almost everybody is a member of a religion, a nation, a family, an association, a political party, or the Rotary or Lions Club. People go on finding more and more chains to bind them. It seems very cozy, and you have so much protection and no responsibility. Freedom, on the other hand, means you will have to be responsible for every act and every breath; whatever you do or don't do, you will be responsible.

People are really in deep fear of freedom, although they talk about freedom. My own experience is that very few people really want freedom, because they are subconsciously aware that freedom will bring many problems they are not ready to deal with. They would rather remain in a cozy imprisonment. The alternative means you have to do something with your freedom. You have to be ready to be a seeker, a searcher, a creator, but very few people want to go on a pilgrimage, or go into deeper silences of the heart, or take the responsibility of love. The implications are great.

You will have to dispel the darkness of sadness, otherwise sooner or later you will enter some prison. You cannot go on burdening yourself with sadness. Before the burden becomes too much and forces you back into some slavery or imprisonment, change the whole situation by being a creative person. Just find out what brings you joy in life, what you would like to create, what you would like to be, and what you want your definition of life to be.

Freedom is simply an opportunity to find a definition for yourself, a true, authentic individuality, and the joy in making the world around you a little better and more beautiful—add a few more roses, a little more greenery, a few more oases.

I am reminded of Madame Blavatsky, the founder of the Theosophical Society. She always used to carry two bags in her hands. Either going for a morning walk or traveling in a train, those two bags were always in her hands. And while sitting on the train from her window she would always throw something out of those bags onto the footpath outside of the train.

> ☙
>
> Freedom is only an opportunity for you. It is not in itself the goal. It simply gives you the whole opportunity to do whatever you want to do. When you are free and you are feeling sad, it is because you have not used this opportunity yet.

And people used to ask, "Why do you go on doing this?"

And she laughed and said, "This has been my whole life's habit.

These are seasonal flower seeds. I may not come back on this route again"—she was a world traveler—"but that does not matter. When the season comes and the flowers blossom, thousands of people who pass this way every day will see those flowers, those colors. They will not know me, but that does not matter.

"One thing is certain: I am making a few people happy somewhere. It does not matter whether they know me or not. What matters is that I have done something that will make someone happy. Some children may come and pluck a few flowers to take home. Some lovers may come and make garlands for each other; and, without their knowing, I will be part of their love. And I will be part of the joy of those children. And I will be part of those who simply pass by the path and see the beautiful flowers."

One who understands that freedom is nothing but an opportunity to make the world a little more beautiful, and to become a little more conscious, will not be sad.

It is good that you asked this question, because if you had not asked, you might have carried on this sadness, which would slowly have poisoned your very freedom. A negative freedom is not very substantial; it can disappear. Freedom has to become positive.

It is possible to to search for the path of truth and free one's own country from tyranny?

There is no conflict between your search for truth, for your spiritual freedom, and your struggle against political tyranny—although matters become a little more complicated.

The priority should be your attainment of spiritual freedom, because political tyrannies come and go. And you cannot be absolutely sure that when you have overthrown one political tyranny, it will not be replaced by another.

No tyranny has ever lasted forever; its days are limited. No one can destroy people's wills. The tyrants can imprison or kill people, but one day they find that their very effort to keep their empire, and keep people enslaved, has turned the people against them.

But what about the new tyrant? You will move from one tyranny into the hands of another. Certainly, the same people will not be killed or sentenced to death. Now the victims will be the people who were involved with the old regime—they will be killed; they will be sentenced to death. But it does not matter who is killed and who is sentenced to death; all are human beings, and all are your brothers and your sisters. And the strangest phenomenon to remember is that even those who have been fighting against the old regime will be shot by the new regime that will replace it.

> Freedom is simply an opportunity to find a definition for yourself, a true, authentic individuality, and a joy in making the world around you a little better, a little more beautiful—

It is a strange fate, but it has a subtle logic in it. Those who have been revolutionaries become accustomed to being revolutionaries; and any regime is antirevolutionary. It may be the regime created by the revolutionaries themselves, but the moment people come into power, they become antirevolutionary, because now revolution goes against their power. They were in favor of revolution, because revolution was bringing power into their hands. This is simple logic. And the revolutionaries cannot believe that this is the freedom they have been fighting for. Only the people have changed, but everything else remains the same: the same bureaucracy, the same ugly politicians.

And these revolutionaries will forget all the promises that they had made to people to get them to support the revolution; they will start exploiting these same people. Naturally, many revolutionaries of the past start drifting away from those who have come into power. Once they were all fighting the enemy, shoulder to shoulder. Now they start drifting away, because the revolution has been betrayed. And now the revolutionaries who have come into power—and power simply destroys all their revolutionary ideologies—start killing the remaining revolutionaries, because they are the most dangerous people. They have overthrown the previous regime; they can overthrow this regime, too.

It is a very complex game. You should not give it priority. Your priority should remain your own growth. It does not matter what kind of tyranny is involved. Tyranny is simply tyranny; it is murderous and criminal.

Don't trust too much in a beautiful future. History teaches us something else. People will remain in the same ugly situation, endure the same horrors under a new regime. Only the butchers have changed.

I am not against fighting for freedom for your nation, but don't make it a priority. Your priority should be for your own spiritual freedom, which cannot be taken away by anyone else. If you can manage to fight against tyranny also at the same time, then I am absolutely in support of it. But I don't think it is easy; in fact, it is very difficult. The moment you start fighting with governments you get so involved that you forget yourself completely.

It is ugly to remain under any kind of slavery. But the greatest slavery is of your soul. Free your soul from the past, free it from the nation, free it from the religion you have been brought up in. Your search for truth should remain your basic and ultimate concern. If you have some energy left, you can go on fighting political tyrannies. But you are going to be disappointed. Everyone down through the ages who had the idea that "We will be free" has been disappointed.

In India, I was a small child when the struggle for freedom was going on, but my whole family was involved in it. My uncles were in jails, my family was almost always under house arrest. My uncles could not complete their education, because the time they were going to spend in the universities was spent in jail instead. And they endured every kind of torture, but there was great hope that this night, however long, would end.

It has ended, but the new day has not come. This is the miracle. The British imperialists have gone, and those who have come into power were those who were fighting against British imperialism and its inhumanity to the people. Now those in power are doing the same things. Certainly this is not the freedom people were hoping for.

> Political tyrannies come and go. And you cannot be absolutely sure that when you have overthrown one political tyranny, it will not be replaced by another.

I remember my childhood days—what great hope there was in the air; it was as if we had come very close to the Golden Age. And except for sheer disappointment, nothing else has happened. Now the rulers are Indians, not Britishers, but their strategies are the same. Their clinging to power is the same; their exploitation of people is the same. The bureaucracy has become stronger, and the country has been in shock. "What happened to the freedom for which we fought? For which our youth was crucified? For which thousands of people were jailed, killed? Is this the freedom for which all these sacrifices were made?"

Certainly, it is not freedom. Perhaps in the political world that kind of freedom can never come unless the rebel is born, not the revolutionary. The revolutionary has failed; and not just one time, but hundreds of times. Now it can be accepted as a rule: the revolutionary talks of great things, promises paradise, and when he comes into power, he proves a greater tyrant than the previous one.

My hope is no longer in the promises of the revolutionaries; my hope is in the birth of the rebel. And a rebel's basic necessity— the essential transformation—is the freedom of your individuality from your own past, from your own religion, from your own nation. Meditation will help to make you an individual; and only a commune of individuals who are all spiritually free, who have broken all the bridges that go back to the past, will have eyes that are fixed on faraway stars.

They are all, in a way, poets, dreamers, mystics, and meditators. And unless we fill the world with these people, the world is just going to exchange one tyranny for another. It will be an exercise in utter futility.

You are the priority. Get to your roots, find yourself, become a rebel, and create as many rebels as possible. That's the only way you can help future mankind create a golden future.

> I am not against fighting for freedom for your nation, but don't give it a priority. The priority should be for your spiritual freedom, which cannot be taken away by anybody else.

The priests and nuns and relatives that shaped my training are now old and dried up. Most are dead. It seems worthless to rebel against those helpless old people.

I am now the priest and the doctrines. I feel that to rebel against anything outside myself is a waste of time and just simply not to the point. This makes the situation much more frustrating and entangled. It seems the self must rebel against the self. I accept that it is not the essential self—the original face—that has to do the rebelling. It is the trained self—the subterfuge. But that is the only "self" I have or know with which to do the rebelling. How does the subterfuge rebel against the subterfuge?

The rebellion I am talking about is not to be done against anybody. It is not really a rebellion, but only an understanding. You are not to fight with the outer priests, nuns, parents. And you are not to fight, either, with the inner priests, nuns, parents. Because outer or inner doesn't matter; they are separate from you. The outer is separate; the inner too is separate. The inner is only the reflection of the outer.

You are perfectly right in saying, "It seems worthless to rebel against those helpless old people." I am not telling you to rebel against them. And I am not telling you, either, to rebel against all that they have put inside you. If you rebel against your own mind it will be a reaction, not a rebellion. Note the difference. A reaction comes out of anger; a reaction is violent. In a reaction you become blind with rage; you start moving to the other extreme.

For example, if your parents have taught you to be clean and take a bath every day, etc., and you have been taught from the very beginning that cleanliness is next to Godliness, and then one day you start rebelling, what will you do? You will stop taking a bath. You will start living in filth. Now you have moved to the other extreme. You were taught cleanliness is next to Godliness; now you are thinking that filthiness is next to Godliness, dirtiness is next to Godliness. From one extreme you have moved to the other. This is not rebellion—this is rage, anger, revenge.

And while reacting to your parents and their so-called ideas of cleanliness, you are still obsessed with that the same idea. It is still haunting you; it still has power over you and is still dominant. It continues to rule your life, although you have chosen the opposite of it. You cannot take a bath easily; you are reminded of your parents who used to force you to bathe every day. Now you don't take a bath at all.

Who is dominating you? Your parents, still. What they have done to you, you have not been able to undo. This is reaction; this is not rebellion.

Then what is rebellion? Rebellion is pure understanding. You simply understand what is the case. Then you are no longer neurotically obsessed with cleanliness, that's all. You don't become unclean. Cleanliness has its own beauty. One should not be obsessed by it, because obsession is sick.

For example, a person continuously washing his hands the whole day is neurotic. The washing of hands is not bad, but just washing them all day long is mad. If instead you stop washing your hands altogether, then again you are trapped in madness.

The person of understanding washes his hands when it is needed. When it is not needed, he is not obsessed by it. He is simply natural and spontaneous about it. He lives intelligently; that's all.

There is not much difference between obsession and intelligence. For example, if you come across a snake on the road and you jump, naturally you jump out of fear. But this fear is intelligence. If you are unintelligent, stupid, then you will not jump out of the way and you will unnecessarily invite danger into your life. The intelligent person will jump immediately—the snake is there. You jump out of fear, but this fear is intelligent, positive, life-serving.

However, this fear can become obsessive. For example, if you cannot sit in a house because you fear it may fall. Houses have been known to fall, that is true. You are not absolutely wrong about that.

You can argue that "If other houses have fallen, why not this one?" Now you are afraid to live under any roof because it may fall down. This is obsession. Now this fear is unintelligent.

One can become obsessive about anything. Anything that may be intelligent within boundaries may become neurotic if you stretch it too far. Reaction is moving to the other extreme. Rebellion is a very deep understanding, a profound understanding, of a certain phenomenon. And rebellion always keeps you in the middle; it gives you balance.

You are not to fight with anyone, nuns or priests or parents, outside or inner. You are not to fight because you will not know when to stop. In a fight, one loses awareness; in a fight, one starts moving to the extreme. You can watch it.

For example, when sitting with your friends you casually say, "That movie I went to yesterday was not worth seeing." You may have mentioned it just in passing, but then somebody says, "You are wrong. I have also seen the movie. It is one of the most beautiful pictures ever made." Now you are provoked, challenged; you become argumentative. You say, "It is worthless, the most worthless thing!" And you start criticizing. And if the other also insists, you become more and more angry and you start saying things you have not even thought about. And later on if you review the whole phenomenon, you will be surprised to note that when you mentioned that the movie was not worth going to, you made a very mild statement, but by the time you finished with the argument, you had moved to the extreme. You had unloosed your whole arsenal of nasty words. You could condemn in any way; you used all your skill of condemnation. And you were not ready to do it in the beginning. If nobody had opposed you, you might have forgotten all about it and might never have made such strong statements. And it happens that when you start fighting you tend to move to the extreme.

I am not teaching you to fight with your conditionings. Understand them. Become more intelligent about them. Just see how they dominate you, how they influence your behavior, how they have shaped your personality, how they go on affecting you. Just watch! Be meditative. And one day, when you have seen the working of your conditionings, suddenly a balance is attained. In your very understanding you are free.

Understanding is freedom, and that freedom I call rebellion.

The real rebel is not a fighter; he is a man of understanding. He simply grows in intelligence, not in anger, nor in rage. You cannot transform yourself by being angry at your past. If you remain angry, then the past will continue to dominate you, it will remain the center of your being, and will remain your focus. And there you will stay, attached to the past. You may switch to the other extreme, but you still will be attached to the past.

Beware of it! That is not the way of a meditator, not the way of rebellion through understanding. Just understand.

You pass by the side of a church

> Reaction is moving to the other extreme. Rebellion is a very deep understanding, profound understanding, of a certain phenomenon. And rebellion always keeps you in the middle, it gives you balance.

and a deep desire arises in you to go inside and pray. Or you pass by the side of a temple and unconsciously you bow down to the deity of the temple. Just watch. Why are you doing these things? I am not saying to fight. I am saying to watch. Why do you bow down to the temple?—because you were taught that this temple is the right temple, that the deity of this temple is the real image of God. Do you know for certain? Or have you just been told that and you have been following it? Watch!

Seeing for yourself that you are just repeating a program that has been given to you, that you are just playing a tape in your head, that you are behaving robot-like, you will now stop bowing automatically. You will not have to make any effort; you will simply forget all about it. That program will disappear, it will leave you without any trace.

In reaction the trace is there. In rebellion there is no trace; it is utter freedom.

And you also ask, "Who is to fight with whom?" Hmm? That question arises only if there has to be a fight. Because there is not going to be a fight, the question does not arise. You just have to be a witness. And the witnessing is your original face; the one who witnesses is your real consciousness. That which is witnessed is conditioning. The one who witnesses is the transcendental source of your being.

Could you please say something more about the fear of freedom? There is such a longing to be free, yet especially recently I see so much fear coming up at the same time. Is it nothing else but avoiding aloneness and responsibility?

This is natural, because from the very beginning of your childhood you have been told to depend on others, their advice, their guidelines. You have grown older, but you have not grown up. All animals grow older. It is only man who has two possibilities: either he can grow old like every other animal, or he can grow up. Growing up means getting rid of all dependence. Naturally, in the beginning it will create fear.

You were surrounded by your own projections, and thinking

that you were protected. For example, you have been told from the very beginning that God is protecting you. Even small children are told in the night, "Don't be afraid. Go to sleep. God is protecting you."

That child is still within you—and I say, "There is no God. You can sleep in darkness in safety. Nobody is protecting you." But that means you cannot sleep; you are afraid, somebody is needed to protect you. That God was hocus-pocus, but it helped. It was like homeopathic medicine—just sugar pills.

But if your disease is just an idea—and there are so many people around who get ideas; just a slight thing and they will exaggerate it, almost unconsciously. No real medicine is needed for their imaginary diseases; all that is needed is an imaginary medicine.

In the first place, darkness is beautiful. It has tremendous depth, silence, infinity. Light comes and goes; darkness always remains, it is more eternal than light. For light you need some fuel; for darkness no fuel is needed—it is simply there. And for relaxing, light is not the right option. Light creates tensions, keeps you awake. Darkness allows you to relax, to let go.

There is no fear in darkness, so the whole idea of fear in darkness is a projection. Then you need a God—another projection—who will protect you in darkness. One lie needs another lie, and then there is no end; you have to go on lying.

Certainly freedom will make you afraid of many things. Be alert. Look deeply into anything that makes you afraid. And you will be surprised that if you look deeply into anything that makes you afraid, it will disappear. There is nothing to fear in the world. Then you can rejoice in freedom and the responsibility it brings.

Responsibility makes you grow up. You become more and more responsible for every action, for every thought, for every feeling. It crystallizes you. It takes away all the chains that have been binding you and your psychology.

I was staying with a friend; we were going to a meeting which I was to address, and the man was driving me there. He was honking the horn for his wife to come down, because we were getting late. And I don't like to be late, because so many people are waiting. It is disrespectful, ungraceful.

Finally his wife looked out of the window and said, "A thousand times I have told you I am coming in a minute!"

I said, "My God! How can she say it a thousand times—and still be coming in a minute?" But she is not conscious of what she is saying.

You have exaggerated your fears. Just look at them, and by looking at them they will lessen. You have never looked at them before; instead you have been trying to escape from them. You have been creating protections against them, rather than looking directly into the eyes of your fear.

There is nothing to fear at all; all that is needed is a little more awareness. So whatever your fear is, catch hold of it, look at it minutely, the way a scientist looks at something. And you will be surprised, it will start melting like a snowflake. By the time you have looked into its totality, it will be gone.

And when freedom is there without any fear, it brings such benediction that there are no words to express it.

How can we help children to grow to their full potential, without imposing our own ideas on them and interfering with their freedom?

The moment you start thinking about how to help children to grow you are already on the wrong track, because whatever you are going to do is going to give the children a certain program. It may be different from the one that you received, but you are conditioning the children—with all the best intentions in the world.

The trees go on growing without anybody teaching them how to grow. The animals, the birds, all of existence needs no programming. The very idea of programming is basically creating slavery— and man has been creating slaves for thousands of years using different names. When people become fed up with one name, another name immediately replaces it. A few modified programs, a few changes here and there in the conditioning, but the fundamental premise remains the same—that the parents, the older generation, want their children to behave in a certain way. That's why you are asking "How?"

According to me, the function of parents is not how to help children grow—they will grow without you. Your function is to support, to nourish, to help what is already growing. Don't give directions and don't give ideals. Don't tell them what is right and what is wrong: let them find it by their own experience.

There is only one thing you can do, and that is to share your own life. Tell them that you have been conditioned by your parents, that you have lived within certain limits, according to certain ideals, and because of these limits and ideals you have missed life completely, and you don't want to destroy their lives. You want them to be totally free—free of you, because to them you represent the whole past.

It takes guts and immense love in a father, in a mother, to tell the children, "You need to be free of us. Don't obey us—depend on your own intelligence. Even if you go astray it is far better than

> Be alert. Look deeply into anything that makes you afraid. And you will be surprised that if you look deeply into anything that makes you afraid, it will disappear.

to remain a slave and always be right. It is better to make mistakes on your own and learn from them, rather than follow someone else and not make mistakes, because then you are never going to learn anything except following—and that is poison, pure poison."

It is very easy if you love. Don't ask "how" because "how" means you are asking for a method, a methodology, a technique—and love is not a technique.

Love your children, enjoy their freedom. Let them make mistakes, help them to see where they have made a mistake. Tell them, "To make mistakes is not wrong—make as many mistakes as possible, because that is the way you will be learning more. But don't make the same mistake again and again, because that makes you stupid."

So I cannot give you a simple answer. You will have to figure it out yourself living with your children from moment to moment, allowing them every possible freedom in small things.

For example, in my childhood—and it has been the same for other children for centuries—I was taught, "Go to bed early, and get up early in the morning. That will make you wise."

I told my father, "It seems strange: when I am not feeling sleepy, you force me to sleep early in the evening." And in Jaina houses early in the evening is really early, because supper is at five o'clock, at the most six. And then there is nothing else to do, so the children are told to go to sleep.

I said to him, "When my energy is not ready to go to sleep, you force me to sleep. And when in the morning I am feeling sleepy, you drag me out of the bed. This seems to be a strange way of making me wise! And I don't see the connection—how am I going to become wise by being forced to sleep when I am not feeling sleepy? And for hours I lie down in the bed, in the darkness—time that would have in some way been used, would have been creative—and you force me to sleep. But sleep is not something in your hands. You cannot just close your eyes and go to sleep. Sleep comes when it comes; it does not follow your order or my order, so for hours I am wasting my time.

"And then in the morning when I am really feeling sleepy, you force me to wake up—five o'clock, early in the morning—and you drag me out for a morning walk towards the forest. I am feeling sleepy and you are dragging me. I don't see how all this is going to make me wise. You please explain it to me!

"How many people have become wise through this process? You just show me a few wise people—I don't see anybody around. And I have been talking to my grandfather, and he said that it is all nonsense. Of the whole household, that old man is the only sincere man. He does not care what others will say, but he has told me that it is all nonsense: 'Wisdom does not come by going early to bed. I have been going early to bed my whole life—seventy years—and wisdom has not come yet, and I don't think it is going to come! Now it is time for death to come, not for wisdom. So don't be fooled by these proverbs.'"

I told my father, "You think it over, and please be fair to me. Give me this much freedom—that I can go to sleep when I feel sleep is coming, and I can get up when I feel that it is time and sleep is no longer there."

He thought it over for one day, and the next day he said,

> The function of the parents is not how to help the children grow—they will grow without you. Your function is to support, to nourish, to help what is already growing. Don't give directions and don't give ideals. Don't tell them what is right and what is wrong: let them find it by their own experience.

"Okay, perhaps you are right. You do it according to your own needs. Listen to your body rather than listen to me."

This should be the <u>principle</u>: <u>children should be helped to listen to their bodies, to listen to their own needs</u>. The basic thing for parents to do is to guard the children from falling into a ditch. The function of their discipline is negative.

Remember the word "negative"—no positive programming but only a negative guarding—because children are children, and they can get into something that will harm or cripple them. Then too don't order them not to go, but explain the situation to them. Don't make it a point of obedience; still let them choose. You simply explain the whole situation.

Children are very receptive, and if you are respectful to them they will be ready to listen, ready to understand. Then leave them with their understanding. And it is a question only of a few years in the beginning; soon they will be getting settled in their intelligence, and your guarding will not be needed at all. Soon they will be able to move on their own.

I can understand the fear of parents that their children may go in a direction they don't like—but that is your problem. <u>Your children are not born to follow your likes and dislikes</u>. They have to live their own life, and you should rejoice that they are doing so— whatever that life is. They may become just poor musicians . . .

I used to know a very rich man who wanted his son, after graduation, to become a doctor. But the son was interested only in music. He was already no longer an amateur; he was well known in the area, and wherever there was any function he could be found playing the sitar. He was becoming more and more famous. He wanted to go to a university that was basically devoted to music. But his father was absolutely against it. He called me—because I was very close to his son—and he said, "He will be a beggar all his life," because musicians in India cannot earn much. "At the most he can become a music teacher in a school. What will he be earning? We pay the servants in our house that much! And he will be associating with the wrong people," because in India, music has remained very deeply connected with prostitutes.

The Indian prostitute is different from any prostitute in the rest of the world. The word "prostitute" does not do justice to the Indian counterpart, because the Indian prostitute is really well versed in music, in dance—and India has so much variety. If you really want to learn the deeper layers of music, singing, and dancing, you have to join with some famous prostitute. There are famous families—they are called *gharanas*. *Gharana* means "family." It is nothing to do with the ordinary family; it is the family of the master-disciple. So there are famous *gharanas* who have a certain way of their own. Presenting the same instrument, the same dance, different *gharanas* will produce it in different ways, with subtle nuances. So, if someone really wants to get into the world of music, he has to join some *gharana*—and that is not good company. According to the rich man, it is certainly not good company.

But the son was not interested in the company. Not following his father, he went to the music university and his father disowned him because he was so angry. And because his father disowned him, and because he had no other way—the university was in a very remote mountainous area where you cannot find any job or anything—he came back and had to become exactly what his father was predicting, just a schoolteacher.

His father called me and reported, "Look, it is just as I have said. My other sons—one is an engineer, one is a professor, but this idiot did not listen to me. I have disowned him; he will not inherit a single cent from me, and now he will remain in just the poorest profession—a schoolmaster."

But my friend himself was immensely happy. He was not worried that he had been abandoned by his family, that he was going to live a poor man's life, that he would not be receiving any inheritance. These things did not bother him; he was happy, "It is good they have done all this—now I can become part of some *gharana*. I was worried about my family, that they would feel humiliated. But now they have abandoned me, and I am no longer part of them, I can become part of some *gharana*."

Teaching in a school, he became part of a *gharana* and is now one of the best musicians in India. It is not a question of his being one of the best musicians; what is important is that he became what he felt was his potential. And whenever you follow your potential, you always become the best. Whenever you go astray from that potential, you remain mediocre.

The whole society consists of mediocre people for the simple reason that nobody is what he was destined to be—he is something else. And whatever he might do, he cannot be the best and he cannot feel fulfillment; he cannot rejoice.

The work of parents is very delicate, and it is precious, because the whole life of the child depends on it. Don't give any positive program—help the child in every possible way to do what he or she wants to do.

> Children are very receptive, and if you are respectful to them they are ready to listen, ready to understand. Then leave them with their understanding. And it is a question only of a few years in the beginning, soon they will be getting settled in their intelligence, and your guarding will not be needed at all.

For example, I used to climb trees. Now, there are a few trees which are safe to climb; their branches are strong, their trunks are strong. You can go even to the very top, and still there is no need to be afraid that a branch will break. But there are a few trees which are very soft. Because I used to climb on the trees to get mangoes and other beautiful fruit, my family was very worried and they would always send somebody to stop me.

I told my father, "Rather than stopping me, please explain to me which trees are dangerous—so that I can avoid them—and which trees are not dangerous, so that I can climb them. But if you try to prevent me from climbing, there is a danger: I may climb a wrong tree, and the responsibility will be yours. I am not going to stop climbing, I love it."

It is really one of the most beautiful experiences to be on the top of the tree in the sun with the high wind, and the whole tree is dancing—a very nourishing experience.

I said, "I am not going to stop climbing. Your work is to tell me exactly which trees I should not climb—because I can fall from them and can suffer fractures, I can damage my body. But don't give me a blanket order to stop climbing. That I am not going to do." My father had to come with me and go around town to show me which trees are dangerous. Then I asked him the second question, "Do you know any good climber in the city who can teach me to climb even the dangerous trees?"

He said, "You are too much! Now this is going too far. You told me and I understood it . . ."

I said, "I will follow your guidance, because I have myself proposed it. But the trees that you are saying are dangerous are irresistible, because jamun"—an Indian fruit—"grows on them. It is really delicious, and when it is ripe I may not be able to resist the temptation. You are my father, it is your duty to help. You must know somebody who can help me."

He said, "If I had known that to be a father was going to be so difficult, I would have never become one—at least not to you! Yes, I know one man." And finally he introduced me to an old man who was a extraordinary climber, the best. He was a tree trimmer, and he was so old that you could not believe that he could do it anymore. He did only rare jobs, which nobody else was ready to do—big trees that were leaning on the houses: he would cut off the dangerous branches. He was an expert, and he did it without damaging the trees' roots or the houses. First he would tie the branches to other branches with ropes. Then he would cut these branches and then with the ropes pull the cut branches away from the house and let them fall on the ground. And he was so old! But whenever there was some situation like that, one which no other woodcutter would do, he was ready.

So my father told him, "Teach this boy something, particularly about trees which are dangerous, which can break." Branches can break . . . and I had fallen already two or three times—I still carry the marks on my legs. That old man looked at me and he said, "Nobody has ever come to ask me this, particularly a father bringing a boy. . . . It is a dangerous thing, but if he loves it, I would love to teach him." And he taught me how to manage to climb trees which were dangerous. He showed me all kinds of strategies of how to protect yourself: If you want to go high up the tree and you don't want to fall onto the ground, then first tie yourself with a rope to a point where you feel the tree is strong enough, and then go up. If you fall, you will be hanging from the rope, but you will not fall to the ground. And that really helped me; since then I have not fallen!

The job of a father or a mother is great, because they are bringing a new guest into the world—one who knows nothing, but who brings some potential. And unless the child's potential grows, he will remain unhappy. No parents like to think of their children remaining unhappy; they want them to be happy. It is just that their usual thinking is wrong. They think if the children become doctors, if they become professors, engineers, or scientists, then they will be happy. They don't know! Children can only be happy if they become what they have come here to become. They can only become the seed that they are carrying within themselves.

So help in every possible way to give freedom, to give opportunities. Ordinarily, if a child asks a mother anything, without even listening to the child, to what he is asking, the mother simply says no. "No" is an authoritative word; "yes" is not. So neither father nor mother nor anybody else who is in authority wants to say yes to any ordinary thing.

The child wants to play outside the house: "No!" The child wants to go out while it is raining and wants to dance in the rain: "No! You will get a cold." A cold is not a cancer, but a child who has been prevented from dancing in the rain, and has never been able again to dance, has missed something great, something really beautiful. A cold would have been worthwhile—and it is not that the child will necessarily catch a cold. In fact, the more you protect him, the more he becomes vulnerable. The more you allow him, the more he becomes immune.

> The work of the parents is very delicate, and it is precious, because the whole life of the child depends on it. Don't give any positive program—help the child in every possible way to do what he or she wants to do.

Parents have to learn to say yes. Ninety-nine times out of a hundred when they ordinarily say no, it is for no other reason than simply to show authority. Everybody cannot become the president of the country with authority over millions of people. But everybody can become a husband, can have authority over his wife; every wife can become a mother, can have authority over the child; every child can have a teddy bear, and have authority over the teddy bear . . . kick him from this corner to the other corner, give him good slaps, slaps that he really wanted to give to the mother or to father. And the poor teddy bear has nobody below him.

This is an authoritarian society. And in creating children who have freedom, who have heard yes and have rarely heard no, the authoritarian society will disappear. We will have a more human society. So it is not only a question of the children. Those children are going to become tomorrow's society: the child is the father of man.

EPILOGUE

THE TRUE FREEDOM IS SPIRITUAL

True freedom has nothing to do with the outside world. True freedom is not political, not economic; it is spiritual. Political freedom can be taken away at any moment; economic freedom can disappear just like a dewdrop in the early morning sun. They are not in your hands. And that which is not in your hands cannot be called true freedom.

True freedom is always spiritual. It has something to do with your innermost being, which cannot be chained, handcuffed, or put into a jail.

Yes, your body can suffer all these things, but your soul is intrinsically free. You don't have to ask for it, and you don't have to struggle for

> What exactly is the innermost substance of freedom?—that you are free from the past, that you are free from the future.

it. It is already there, this very moment. If you turn inwards, all chains, all prisons, all kinds of slaveries disappear—and there are many. Freedom is only one; slaveries are many—just as truth is one, lies can be thousands.

What exactly is the innermost substance of freedom?—that you are free from the past, that you are free from the future. You do not have memories binding you with the past, dragging you always backwards—that is against existence; nothing goes backwards. And your freedom comes also from imagination, desire, longing—they drag you towards the future.

Neither the past exists nor the future exists. All that you have in your hands is the present. And one who lives in the present, unburdened of past and future, knows the taste of freedom. There are no chains—chains of memories, chains of desires. These are the real chains which bind your soul and never allow you to live the moment that is yours.

As far as I am concerned, I cannot see that one can ever be free without a meditative mind.

In India what is known in the West as paradise is known as *moksha. Moksha* means "freedom." Paradise does not mean freedom, paradise comes from a Persian root, *phirdaus,* which means "a walled garden." But don't forget that it is a *walled* garden: it may be a garden, but it is a prison.

The biblical story says that God became annoyed with Adam and Eve and threw them out of the Garden of Eden. Into what? Where? If you ask me, this was a curse that was hiding the greatest freedom, the greatest blessing. Adam and Eve were let out of the prison, and that was the beginning of humanity. Now the whole sky and the whole earth was theirs, and it was up to them what to make of it. It is unfortunate that they have not been able to create a free world. Each nation has again become a walled prison—not even a walled garden.

In a small school, the religious teacher was talking to the children about the biblical beginnings of the world. A small boy raised his hand to ask a question. The teacher said, "What is your question?"

He said, "My question is, the Bible says that God drove out Adam and Eve. What model of car did he use?"

It must have been a Ford—the first model, called the Model-T Ford. And I think that poor God is still driving the Model-T Ford—and without any mechanics, because neither is his son Jesus Christ a mechanic, nor is the Holy Ghost, nor is he himself.

Christianity thinks that God punished man. My understanding and insight says that God may have thought he was punishing them, but the reality is that God is still imprisoned in a walled garden. And it was a blessing in disguise that he made man free. His intention was not good, but the result was the whole evolution of humankind. And if evolution is not going as fast as it should go, again the priests of God, of all religions, are preventing it.

When Galileo found that it is not the sun that goes around the earth, that it is an appearance and not a reality—when he found that reality is just the opposite; the earth goes around the sun—he wrote a treatise explaining his reasons, evidence, proofs, arguments. He was very old—seventy or seventy-five—and sick, bedridden, almost dying. But Christian love is such that people representing the church dragged him from his bed to the court of the pope.

The pope said, "You have committed the gravest crime, because the Bible says, and everybody knows, that the sun goes around the earth. Either you have to change your opinion, or death will be the penalty."

Galileo, even in his old age, sick and dying, must have been an immensely beautiful man, a man with a sense of humor. He said, "Your Holiness, there is no problem. I can write what you are saying. There is just one thing I want to make clear to you—that my writing is going to be read neither by the sun nor by the earth. They will continue in their old way, as they have always done. The earth will continue to go around the sun. You can burn my book or I can change the paragraph."

The pope said, "You change the paragraph."

He changed the paragraph and wrote, "According to the Bible and according to the pope and according to the ordinary humanity, it appears that the sun goes around the earth." And in the footnote he wrote, "The truth is just the opposite. I cannot help it—I cannot convince the earth and the sun to follow the Bible. They are not Christian." The footnote was discovered only after his death; otherwise he would have been crucified by the Christians—who go on making so much fuss about the crucifixion of Jesus.

> *What religions lack is courage—courage to be on the side of truth. And it is not only Christians, the case is the same with the Hindus, the Mohammedans, the Jews, the Buddhists, the Jainas. There is not any difference in their mentality.*

I was talking to one of the most influential Christian missionaries in India, Stanley Jones, and I asked him, "What do you think about it? Why was the pope so insistent? If science had discovered it, the Bible should have been corrected."

Stanley Jones said to me, "It might have great implications. If one statement in the Bible is wrong, then what is the guarantee that other statements are not wrong?" The Bible is a holy book, coming directly from God. Nothing can be changed in it, nothing can be edited out, nothing can be added into it. And in the last three hundred years man has found so many things which are against the Bible.

In fact, as you grow in consciousness, you are bound to find that what was written two thousand years ago, or five thousand years ago, has to be continually improved. New editions have to be produced. But what religions lack is courage—courage to be on the side of truth. And it is not only Christians, the case is the same with the Hindus, the Mohammedans, the Jews, the Buddhists, the Jainas. There is not any difference in their mentality.

A man of freedom is free of the past. And the man of freedom is also free of the future, because you don't know what is going to happen the next moment. How can you go on desiring?

An old man was dying. His four sons, who used to live in different houses, were immensely rich people. Hearing that their father was dying, they rushed to him.

The father was dying, taking his last breath on the bed, and just sitting by the side of the bed, the sons started discussing how to take his body to the graveyard. Their concern was not the father—a few minutes more and he would be gone, forever; there was no possibility of their meeting or recognizing each other again . . . but that was not their concern. Their concern was, "When he dies, how are we going to transport his body?"

The youngest boy suggested, "He always wanted to have a Rolls Royce. And he has enough money, we have enough money; there is no need for him to suffer and re-press an innocent desire. So at least we should bring a Rolls Royce to carry his body to the graveyard. In his life he missed having one, but at least in death he will have the Rolls Royce."

The second boy said, "You are too young and you don't understand matters concerning money. It is a sheer waste. He is dead—whether you take him in a Rolls

Royce or in a truck does not matter to him. He will not be able to know about it, so why waste money?" And it was not much money either, just to hire a Rolls Royce. It was not a question of purchasing it. He said, "My suggestion is that a cheap truck will do as efficiently as any Rolls Royce—for the dead it makes no difference."

The third boy said, "You are also still immature. Why bother about a truck, when the municipal sanitation department takes, free of charge, any beggar who dies? Just put him out on the road! In the morning the municipal truck, with all kinds of rubbish, will take him for free. Give him a free ride! And what does it matter to a dead man whether it is a municipal truck or a hired truck or a Rolls Royce?"

> If you have thrown out all the rubbish of the past and all the desires and ambitions for the future, this very moment you are free—just like a bird on the wing, the whole sky is yours.

At that very moment the old man opened his eyes and said, "Where are my shoes?" They were puzzled, "What are you going to do with shoes? You are going to die."

He said, "I'm still alive and perhaps I have a few more breaths. Just bring the shoes; I will walk to the graveyard. That is the cheapest and the sanest way. You are all extravagant, spendthrifts."

People may have money, and the money becomes their fetter. People may have prestige, and the prestige becomes their fetters. It seems the whole past of humanity has been improving on how to make better chains, but even if a chain is made of gold, it is still a chain. Freedom on the outside is just the politician's continuous deceiving of the whole humanity.

Freedom is your individual affair. It is totally subjective. If you have thrown out all the rubbish of the past and all the desires and ambitions for the future, this very moment you are free—just like a bird on the wing, the whole sky is yours. Perhaps even the sky is not the limit.

But man is so much in love with his own misery that he cannot understand the idea of freedom—because to be free is to be free of misery. And it seems that man is afraid to be free. He wants some father in the sky, at least for complaints and prayers. He needs a father in the sky as God, to take care of him. Without God in the sky, he feels like a lost child. It is a father fixation, psychologically. Because you need a father figure, you invent a God who takes care of you. It is your invention—in a certain way you worship yourself, in a roundabout way. Simpler would have been to just put a mirror up, stand before the mirror and with folded hands, repeat any kind of prayer—Hebrew, Sanskrit, Arabic, Greek, Latin. Don't use the language that you know, because when you know the language your prayer looks very ordinary. When you don't know the language, it is mystifying.

Your worship is just like slaves praising the tyrant who has reduced them from humanity into slavery. And he can kill them at any moment, because a slave is property, not a person. Thousands of years of many kinds of slavery have made you so afraid to be free—which is your birthright and which is your ultimate blissfulness. Your so-called temples and synagogues and mosques and churches are not symbols of freedom, they are symbols of your slavery, of your dead tyrants. But even intelligent people go on doing the same thing. Man's blindness seems to be unlimited.

So for thousands of years, if you have been in chains, handcuffed, you must have started believing that these are ornaments, that this is the will of God. Your parents cannot be your enemies. If they take you to the church or to the temple, they take you there because they love you. But the reality is, they take you there because they were taken there by their parents. It is a robot-like process, mechanical. And slowly, slowly the slavery has penetrated into your blood, into your bones, into your very marrow.

So if somebody speaks against Krishna, immediately you are ready to fight with him: he has spoken against your God—who is nothing but a slavery. If somebody speaks against Jesus, immediately you are furious, he has spoken against your God—but he was speaking only against your chains.

This is the reason why I have been condemned by all the countries of the world, all the religions of the world—because I'm speaking against their slavery. It is polished, decorated, and they have always lived in it. Their parents and their parents' parents . . . long line of slaves. How can they drop their inheritance? You get in inheritance nothing but slavery. And even if you don't take it seriously, still it is serious.

I have heard:

Three rabbis were talking about their synagogues. The first rabbi said, "My synagogue is the most advanced because in my synagogue, while I am delivering the sermon, people are allowed to smoke, gossip, talk. I have given them total freedom."

The other two rabbis laughed. The second one said, "This you call advancement? Come to my synagogue. I have given them freedom to drink alcohol, and when they become drunk they shout, they scream, they fight, but I continue giving my discourse. This is freedom."

In a synagogue women and men cannot sit together; there is a curtain between them. And the second rabbi also said, "The curtain has been removed. Now women and men sit together. I don't even interfere . . . whether it is your wife you are sitting with or not. Even boyfriends and girlfriends are allowed to do all kinds of loving things—kissing, hugging—and my discourse continues. We have entered into the era of freedom."

The third rabbi said, "You are both idiots. You should come sometime to my synagogue. I have placed a board in front of the synagogue, saying that on every Jewish holiday the synagogue will remain closed. This is freedom. Why waste people's time? At least on a holiday let them have all kinds of entertainment available to them."

But these are not freedoms. They are all still Jews. Unless you drop your Jewishness, your Hinduism, your Jainism, your Mohammedanism, unless you are completely clean of the past, unless you are no longer dominated by the dead and no longer enchanted by the unpredictable future, you are not free. Freedom is here and now—neither the yesterday nor the tomorrow, but this very moment.

A man of understanding unburdens himself. And all the chains that have been heavy on his heart—although he had become accustomed to that heaviness- -disappear.

I am saying it to you with absolute authority, because it is my experience. The moment your chains disappear you start growing wings for the sky. Then the whole sky, full of stars, is yours.

But remember: The very desire for freedom can also become a fetter. All desires fetter you; freedom is not an exception, for the simple reason that all desires live in the future. One who is really free does not even know anything about slavery or freedom, he enjoys his freedom. It is his very quality of being.

All goals are bound to be in the future, and all desires for fulfillment in the future are nothing but a cover-up of your misery in the present. Your tomorrows go on giving you promises—"It is only one day, it will pass; tomorrow I will be free." But tomorrow never comes, has never come. You will never be free. Tomorrow is only a consolation. Instead of bringing freedom to you, it is going to bring death to you. And all the days that you lived, you lived as a slave, because you never bothered about the present.

I say to you that the present is the only reality there is. The future is your imagination, and the past is your memory. They don't exist. What exists is the present moment. To be fully alert in the present, to gather your consciousness from past and future and concentrate in the present, is to know the taste of freedom.

But it seems man has fallen into such a trap. He is not even as free as the birds of the sky, or the wild animals of the forest. There are so many fetters around him, and he has accepted them.

In fact, what is your care right now? What is your anxiety right now? What is your anguish right now? In this silence, you are absolutely free.

If the whole day you are disturbed and worried, and hankering and desiring, and feeling frustrated, your nights will be nightmares. But if you are living each moment in its totality, with intensity, with your wholeness, your nights will be calm and quiet, relaxed and peaceful. Not even a dream can disturb you, because dreams come from unfulfilled life, from repressed life.

Western psychologists have missed the point completely—particularly psychoanalysts; they go on analyzing your dreams without bothering about the source. The source is in your waking hours—but you are so fettered, so imprisoned in your religion, in your morality, in your etiquette, in your manners, that you cannot live. All these unlived moments will return to you when you are asleep, because anything unlived slips into your unconscious. If you are living fully . . .

Freud would have been very much surprised to know, if he had come to the East, and gone to see the aboriginals who live deep in the forests. I have visited them, and the most surprising thing was that they don't have any dreams. They know the real depth and relaxation of life. Naturally, in the morning they are more alive, more young, more fresh, to face the day and to live it again totally. The condition of the civilized man is just the opposite. He does not only dream in the night. Anytime, sit in your chair, relax, and close your eyes, and some dream starts floating by.

You are not living. You are only desiring to live. You are hoping to live someday, hoping that this night is not going to last forever, that sometime there must be a dawn. But for the slave there is no dawn. He has to live in darkness, without even becoming aware that there is such a thing as light.

Don't take your so-called life for granted. This is not life at all. You have to go through a revolution; and that revolution has nothing to do with any politics, with any economics. It has something to do with your spirituality, and an awareness—when your innermost core is full of light, your outer light also starts reflecting it.

Because your old habits are old, and old companions to you, they will again and again try to make you unfree. But you should be aware always to transcend them. You should watch them coming, and say to them good-bye forever. That is, to me, the essential meaning of sannyas. Then suddenly you become part of these beautiful trees . . . with beautiful roses, with great stars—they are all free.

Except in man, there exists no slavery in the world. And to get out of it is not difficult. It is not a question of your slavery clinging to you. The reality is: you are clinging to your slavery. Your chains are your responsibility. You have accepted them; they are there.

In full awareness, say to them, "Good-bye, you have been long with us. It is enough, we depart." A simple awareness is needed to bring freedom to you, but there are some vested interests in clinging to your slavery.

I was a teacher in the university, and for almost twenty days each month I was out of the town, moving around the country. That much leave is not possible; even though within ten days each month I was completing the course with the students. I asked them, "Have you any complaint?"

They said, "We are grateful to see the fact that for a small course, two years are wasted . . . not more than six months are needed." But the vice-chancellor became disturbed, because again and again he found that I was not in the university.

I had my own device. There had been beautiful trees around the university campus, but strangely, all the trees had died. There was only one tree that was still green and with shade, so I used to park my car under that tree. It had become known that nobody else should park his car there. Once or twice, people had tried, and I had called my students to remove the car . . . "Wherever it goes, let it go, but this place is reserved." So whenever I was going out of town, I used to send my car with my chauffeur, and the vice-chancellor, seeing my car under the tree from his window, was satisfied that I was there.

One day he was taking a round of the whole university, and he found my class was empty. He asked the students, "He is supposed to be here, and his car is parked right under the tree. In fact, I have been always suspicious: I have been reading his discourses—sometimes in Calcutta, sometimes in Amritsar, sometimes in Madras— and I have always been puzzled; his car is here."

I used to drive my car, and I had told my chauffeur, "Lock the car and enjoy yourself for one or two hours in the garden, and then take the car back home."

He said, "What is the point?"

I said, "Don't be worried about it; it is not your problem."

So when I came back from Madras one day, the vice-chancellor called me and asked, "It seems you are your own master. You never ask for leave, you never even inform me."

I said, "Just give me a piece of paper," and I resigned.

He said, "What are you doing?"

I said, "That is my answer. Are my students, in any way, suffering by my absence? Have they said to you that their courses are not complete? It is sheer nonsense to waste their two years. My job is to teach them their full course. It does not matter how many days I take to do it."

In the evening he came to my house, and he said, "Don't leave us."

I said, "What has happened, has happened, and I cannot go back to your university for the simple reason that I have burned all my certificates. I don't want bridges with the past. I will never need these certificates. Now I am an uneducated man."

He said, "I will not say anything to anybody about the certificates."

I said, "That is not the point. I really wanted to resign, but I was simply waiting—it should come from you, not from me."

My father was worried, my friends were worried. My students came, saying, "Please take your resignation back."

I said, "That is impossible. I don't have any qualifications to be your teacher anymore."

My father said to me, "Even if you have resigned, what is the point of burning all your certificates and qualifications?"

I said, "What is the point of keeping them? Keeping them means that somewhere deep down, the desire is still there . . . perhaps you may need them, cling to them. I am now completely free of all that education, which has not given anything to me. They are not certificates, they are wounds—and I don't want to carry those wounds always with me."

After two years, the vice-chancellor asked me, "At least once in a while you can come to address the whole university." So I went.

He took me into his room, to the window from where he used to see my car. He said, "A strange phenomenon—only that tree was green. Now that too has died."

I said, "Life is mysterious. Perhaps the tree had fallen in love with me, because for nine years my car was waiting there and I had become very friendly with the tree." It was not only a question of parking the car under it, I always thanked the tree. Once in a while, when my chauffeur was with me, sitting at the back, he would say, "You are really crazy—thanking the tree?"

I said, "The tree is so loving. Out of all the trees in the line, it is a very beautiful tree"—a gulmarg, with red flowers. When spring comes you can hardly see the leaves; there are so many flowers that the whole tree becomes red. The same kind of trees had all died, but she remained with me alive for nine years. Now somebody else parks his car there, but perhaps he never even bothered to thank the tree, had never shown his gratitude to the tree.

The moment you are free of past and future, just sit by the side of a tree, whisper something to the tree, and soon you will know that it responds. Of course, its response is not going to be in words; perhaps it showers its flowers on you; perhaps it dances in the wind. And if you are sitting very close, your back touching the tree, you will start feeling a certain new sensation that you have never felt before. The tree is vibrating with love for you.

This whole existence is full of love, full of freedom—except the miserable human being. And nobody is responsible for it except you. And it is not a question of gradually dropping those things that make you miserable. Many people have come to me and said, "We understand you; gradually we will drop our miseries." But slavery is never dropped gradually: either you have understood and you are free, or you have not understood and are just pretending to understand.

Freedom does not come in fragments, neither does slavery go

in fragments. When you bring a light into a dark room, have you not seen it? Does the darkness go in fragments—a little part, then another part, making a queue, going out of the room? Or does the light come in fragments—a little light, then more, then more? No, the moment you bring the light in, there is no darkness.

In the very understanding of what freedom is . . . you are free. It is not a question of time, or gradualness.

There is no other way but to drop your chains all together. All those chains you started creating around yourself in your very childhood. Perhaps in the name of obedience, in the name of your love for your parents, in the name of trust in your priests, in the name of respect for your teachers—good names. Always remember to remove the label and see what the content is inside, and you will be surprised: <u>slavery is being sold to every child in beautiful</u> names. It will be difficult for you to drop that, unless you see that it was not the slavery that you were attached to, it was the label that was given to it.

> A human being's life is small. Be decisive about it: You have to be free in your soul, because that is the only freedom there is.

It was a constant fight with my father. He was a loving man, very understanding, but still he would say, "You have to do it." And my response would always be, "You cannot say to me, 'You have to do it,' you can only suggest, 'If you like, you can do it; if you don't like, you are free.' It has to be basically my decision, not yours. I am obedient towards the truth, towards freedom. I can sacrifice everything for truth, for freedom, for love, but not for any slavery. Your 'should' stinks of slavery."

Soon he understood that I don't belong to the obedient or the disobedient. I am not saying, "I will not do it," I am simply saying, "Withdraw your 'should.' Give me space to decide whether I want to say yes or no, and don't feel offended if I say no.

"It is my life, I have to live it, and I have every right to live in my own way. You are much more experienced; you can suggest, you can advise, but orders I am not going to take from anyone. Whatsoever the cost, whatsoever the consequence, orders I am not going to take from anyone."

And slowly, slowly he dropped his "should." He started saying, "There is this problem. If you feel right, you can help me; if you don't feel like helping, it is your decision."

I said, "This is what real love should be."

What do you call freedom?—mostly the political, the economic, the outside freedom, which is not in your hands, which has been given to you. It can be taken away. Only that which has grown within you cannot be taken away from you.

A human being's life is small. Be decisive about it: You have to be free in your soul, because that is the only freedom there is.

☙

Man is born with a soul, but not with a self.

Although all the dictionaries will be saying that these two words, "soul" and "self," are synonymous, it is not true. Soul you bring with you. The self is created by the society as a substitute so that you need not feel without identity . . . because the search for the soul may take long years of pilgrimage, of seeking and searching, and it will be impossible to bear a namelessness, an emptiness, a nobodiness.

The intention to create the self was out of love, so that from the very beginning you start feeling who you are; otherwise how will you live? How will you be addressed? The people who created the idea of the self were full of good intentions, but because they themselves had no idea of their own souls, they created a false self and they died as a created self. They never came to know what existence has made them, and for what.

Your soul is part of existence. Your self is a social institution. So the first thing to remember is that the distinction is unbridgeable. If you want to seek and know who you really are, you will have to go through a radical change of destroying your own self. If you don't destroy the self, and by some accident you come to discover the soul, you will not be one. That's what is called "schizophrenia" by psychologists. You will be split. Sometimes you will behave like the self, and sometimes like a soul. You will be in a constant tension. Your life will become simply a deep anguish and anxiety—and it is impossible to live such a life. Hence society, the educational system, parents, the priest—everybody around you, tries in every way to create such a strong self that you never become aware of the hidden soul.

The journey is not long, but certainly very arduous. The self is not a simple thing—it is very complex. You are a professor, you are a doctor, you are a lawyer, you are a president; you are beautiful, you are very knowledgeable, you are rich, you are ambitious—all these dimensions are of the self. And the self goes on accumulating more money, more power, more prestige, more respectability—its ambition is unfulfillable. You go on and on creating more and more layers of self.

This is the misery of man, the basic misery. Man does not know who he is, yet he goes on believing that he is this, he is that. If you are a doctor, that is your function, not your reality; if you are a president, that is your function, just as somebody else's function is to make shoes. Neither the shoemaker nor the prime minister knows his real self. Parents start from the very beginning, from the very first day. And this false ego, self, or whatever you call it, almost becomes your reality, and the real is forgotten.

The English word "sin" is very significant—not in the sense Christians use it, not in the sense it is being understood all over the world, but in its very roots the word comes with a totally different meaning. It means forgetfulness. It has nothing to do with your action, it has something to do with your reality that you have forgotten.

Because you have forgotten your reality, and you are living with a false substitute, all your actions become hypocritical. You smile, but the smile is not coming from your heart. You weep, you cry, but the tears are very superficial. You love, but your love has no roots in your being. All your actions are as if you are a somnambulist—a person who walks in his sleep.

This happened in New York: There are so many people, somnambulists, that you would not believe—10 percent of humanity. They get up in the night, they go to the fridge; they eat something that the doctor has forbidden them, because they are getting fatter and fatter and creating their own death, committing a slow suicide. In the day somehow they manage to repress it, but in the night the conscious mind is fast asleep and the unconscious does not miss the opportunity. It knows the way—and they walk with open eyes; even in the dark they don't stumble.

They are worried, their doctor is worried, their family is worried: "We have reduced your food, we are not giving you any sugar, and still you go on becoming fat!" And they are also worried that things go on disappearing from the fridge. And you cannot hold that person responsible, because he doesn't remember anything at all in the morning.

But this New York case became world-famous. This man used to live in a fifty-story building, on the top story. In the night he would get up, go to the terrace and jump across to the other house, which was close by. The distance was such that nobody could have dared, with consciousness, to take such a jump—and it was an everyday routine!

Soon people became aware and started gathering underneath

to see, because it was almost a miracle. The crowd started becoming bigger and bigger, and one day, when the man was just about to jump, the crowd shouted loudly, hailing the man. That made him wake up. But it was too late—he had taken the jump. He could not reach the other terrace—although each day he had been going to the other terrace, coming back, going back to his room and falling asleep. But because he became conscious and he saw what he was doing. . . . But he had already taken the jump. He fell down from fifty stories and his body was shattered in fragments on the road.

Your false self is your sleep. The soul is your awakening.

And to keep the self, society has given you certain rules and disciplines. For example, every small child is made ambitious. Nobody says to anybody, "Just be yourself." Everybody is giving him great ideals: "Be a Gautam Buddha or a Jesus Christ or an Albert Einstein . . . but be someone! Don't just go on remaining yourself—you are nothing." Your self needs many degrees, your self needs recognitions, honor. Those are its nourishment; it lives on them. And even the people who renounce the world—become sannyasins, monks—do not renounce their selves. It is easy to renounce the world; it is very difficult to renounce the self because you don't know anything else about yourself. You know your business, you know your education, you know your name—and you know perfectly well you had come without a name. You had come a *tabula rasa*; nothing was written on you, and your parents and your teachers and your priests started writing all over you.

You go on believing in the self for your whole life. And it is very touchy because it is very thin—thin in the sense that it is false. That's why the egoist is such a touchy person.

I used to go for a morning walk when I was a teacher in the university. I had no idea who he was, but there was an old man, and just because of his age I used to say, "Good morning," to him—and we were the only two persons at that early hour, three o'clock in the morning. One day I forgot to say good morning to the man, and he said, "Hey, have you forgotten?"

I said, "This is strange! I don't know you at all; it was just out of sheer courtesy towards an older man, who was as old as my grandfather, that I would say good morning to you. But it is not a contract, such that I have to do it every day." He was demanding it because it had become a fulfillment of a certain part of his self. I had no idea who he was, but he had every idea about me, and it was hurting to him that I had not said, "Good morning, sir."

I said, "I will never say it again to you—or to any old man—just out of courtesy, because I was poisoning your mind."

Have you ever thought about it? You have entered the world without a name, but if somebody says something against your name you will be ready to fight—without even thinking that you have come into world without a name; this name is a false label. You don't have any name—namelessness is your reality.

People who renounce the world are worshiped as saints, but nobody sees that their egos have become even more subtle, stronger than ever before.

I have heard:

There were three Christian monasteries deep in the hills, and one day three monks, one from each monastery, just by chance met on the road. They were tired—they had been coming from the city—so they rested under a tree. The first monk said, "I am proud of my monastery. We may not be as knowledgeable as the people who live in your monasteries, but you cannot compete with us as far as living in austerity is concerned."

The second monk laughed. He said, "Forget all about austerities!—austerity is nothing but torturing yourself. The real thing is the knowledge of your ancient scriptures. Nobody can compete with us. Our monastery is the oldest, and we have all the scriptures, and our people are so scholarly. What about austerities?—that you fast, that you don't eat in the night, that you eat only one time a day. How dare you?—all these things can be done by any idiot. But what wisdom have you gained?"

The third monk was listening silently. He said, "You both may be right. One lives in a very arduous and hard way, sacrificing his body; and the other may also be right— that his people are great scholars."

They both asked, "But what about you and your monastery?"

He said, "What about me and my monastery? We are the tops in humbleness."

Tops in humbleness! It is so difficult . . . Now they have grown, for their self, a religious garment. It has become stronger. Hence I say even sinners may have reached to the ultimate shores of life, but not the saints . . . because the sinner knows he is neither living in austerity, nor is he knowledgeable, nor is he humble; he is just an ordinary person who knows nothing. And perhaps he is the person who is more religious because he is less of a self, and coming closer to his soul.

The real freedom is neither political, nor economic, nor social; the real freedom is spiritual. If it were not so, then Ramakrishna could not have become what he became—a light unto himself— because at the time, India was living under the slavery of the British rulers. Then Raman Maharshi would not have been such a glory, such a silence and such a blessing, because British imperialism was still keeping the country in slavery.

Spiritual freedom cannot be touched.

Your self can be made a slave, but not your soul. Your self is sellable, but not your soul. If you want to know what real freedom is, you will have to go on dropping fragments of your self—forgetting that you are a Brahmin and not a sudra; forgetting that you are a Christian, not just a human being; forgetting what your name is—knowing it is only an ordinary utility but not your reality; forgetting all your knowledge—knowing that it is all borrowed, it is not your own experience, your own attainment.

The whole world may be full of light, but deep inside you are living in darkness. What use is the world full of light, when you don't even have a small flame inside you, slowly, slowly trying to understand that whatever has been added to you after your birth is not your true reality?

And as fragments of the self disappear you start becoming aware of an enormous sky, as vast as the sky outside . . . because existence is always in balance. The outer and the inner are in harmony and in balance. Your self is not that which is confined to your body; your real soul is that which will not be burned even if your body is burned.

Krishna is right when he says, "No weapon can even touch me and neither can the fire burn me." He is not talking about the body, the brain, the self—they will all be destroyed—but there is something in you that is indestructible, immortal, eternal. It was with you before your birth and it will be with you after your birth, because it is you, your essential being.

To know it is to be free, free from all prisons: the prisons of the body, the prisons of the mind, the prisons that exist outside you.

Just live your life with as much joy and celebration, as a gift of existence. Dance with the trees in the sun, in the rain, in the wind. Neither do the trees have any scriptures, nor do the animals have any scriptures; neither do the stars have any scriptures, nor do they have any saints. Except man, nobody is obsessed with the dead. This obsession I call one of the greatest mistakes that has been committed over thousands of years. It is time it should be stopped completely.

For each new generation, leave the space open to search, to find the truth, because finding the truth is less blissful than searching for it. The pilgrimage is the real thing, not the reaching to the temple. Help your children to be proud, not obedient, not slaves. Help them to be free. Teach them that there is no higher value than freedom of living and freedom of expression. Make them capable . . . that if the need arises it is better to die than to accept any kind of slavery.

But this is not being done. And unless it is done you cannot save the world from the Adolf Hitlers, Joseph Stalins, Mao Tse-tungs, Ronald Reagans—you cannot save humanity from tyrants, dictators. In fact, deep down you desire them. Deep down you want somebody to dictate the terms and style of your life. You are so afraid of making mistakes . . . because if you are free, naturally you will make many mistakes. But remember, that is the way of life.

Many times you will fall. There is no harm in this. Get up again and learn not to fall. Be more alert. You will make mistakes, but don't make the same mistake again. This is how

> Not a single person is born in the world who has not a certain capacity which will make him proud, who is not pregnant with something to produce, to give birth to something new and beautiful, to make the existence richer. There is not a single person who has come into the world empty.

one becomes wise. This is how one becomes an individual, proud like a cedar tree rising high, reaching to the stars.

Don't be a pygmy. Try to reach to the ultimate height of which you are capable.

And I say unto you that not a single person is born in the

world who has not a certain capacity which will make him proud, who is not pregnant with something to produce, to give birth to something new and beautiful, to make the existence richer. There is not a single person who has come into the world empty.

Have you seen children when they are born? Their hands are closed. A closed hand, a fist, is a mystery: one never knows what is hidden inside. And have you seen the dead man? When somebody dies . . . have you seen any dead man with a fist? It is impossible. A dead man dies with an open hand, empty, spent. These are only metaphors. I am saying a child is born full of possibilities—he need not be jealous of anyone.

As you go beyond the false self, you suddenly discover a sky that has no limits. A few have called it God, a few have called it Brahma, but the best word is used by Mahavira and Gautam Buddha: they have called it *moksha. Moksha* means "total freedom"— freedom from all that binds you, freedom from all that is false, freedom from all that is going to die. And as you become free from all that is false and mortal, immediately doors of immortality open for you.

I hope that none of you misses that dance, that song, that music of eternity.

About the Author

Osho's teachings defy categorization, covering everything from the individual quest for meaning to the most urgent social and political issues facing society today. His books are not written but are transcribed from audio and video recordings of extemporaneous talks given to international audiences over a period of thirty-five years. Osho has been described by the *Sunday Times* in London as one of the "1,000 Makers of the 20th Century" and by American author Tom Robbins as "the most dangerous man since Jesus Christ."

About his own work Osho has said that he is helping to create the conditions for the birth of a new kind of human being. He has often characterized this new human being as "Zorba the Buddha"—capable of enjoying both the earthy pleasures of a Zorba the Greek and the silent serenity of a Gautam Buddha. Running like a thread through all aspects of Osho's work is a vision that encompasses both the timeless wisdom of the East and the highest potential of Western science and technology.

Osho is also known for his revolutionary contribution to the science of inner transformation, with an approach to meditation that acknowledges the accelerated pace of contemporary life. His unique "Active Meditations" are designed to first release the accumulated stresses of body and mind, so that it is easier to experience the thought-free and relaxed state of meditation.

OSHO® Meditation Resort

The Osho Meditation Resort is a place where people can have a direct personal experience of a new way of living with more alertness, relaxation, and fun. Located about one hundred miles southeast of Mumbai in Pune, India, the resort offers a variety of programs to thousands of people who visit each year from more than a hundred countries around the world.

Originally developed as a summer retreat for maharajas and wealthy British colonialists, Pune is now a thriving modern city that is home to a number of universities and high-tech industries. The meditation resort spreads over forty acres in a tree-lined suburb known as Koregaon Park. The resort campus provides accommodation for a limited number of guests, and there is a plentiful variety of nearby hotels and private apartments available for stays of a few days up to several months.

Resort programs are all based on the Osho vision of a qualitatively new kind of human being who is able both to participate creatively in everyday life and to relax into silence and meditation. Most programs take place in modern, air-conditioned facilities and include a variety of individual sessions, courses, and workshops covering everything from creative arts to holistic health treatments, personal transformation and therapy, esoteric sciences, the "Zen" approach to sports and recreation, relationship issues, and significant life transitions for men and women. Individual sessions and group workshops are offered throughout the year, alongside a full daily schedule of meditations.

Outdoor cafes and restaurants within the resort grounds serve both traditional Indian fare and a choice of international dishes, all made with organically grown vegetables from the commune's own farm. The campus has its own private supply of safe, filtered water.

For more information about Osho and his work, see:

www.osho.com

This is a comprehensive Web site in several languages, featuring an online tour of the meditation resort, a calendar of its course offerings, a catalog of books and tapes, a list of Osho information centers worldwide, and selections from Osho's talks.

Or contact:

Osho International
New York
e-mail: oshointernational@oshointernational.com

OSHO®

LOOK WITHIN...

TAO: THE PATHLESS PATH

Contemporary interpretations of selected parables from the *Lieh Tzu* reveal how the timeless wisdom of this 2500-year-old Taoist classic contains priceless insight for living today.

ISBN: 1-58063-225-4   Paperback $11.95/$17.95 Can.

YOGA: THE SCIENCE OF THE SOUL

Modern yoga emphasizes physical postures and exercises to increase flexibility and aid in relaxation. But yoga has its roots in the understanding of human consciousness and its potential. Explore this potential with Osho's unique insights into yoga and its relationship to the modern mind.

ISBN: 0-312-30614-8   Paperback $12.95/$18.95 Can.

ZEN: THE PATH OF PARADOX

"Zen is not a philosophy, it is poetry. It does not propose, it simply persuades. It does not argue, it simply sings its own song. It is aesthetic to the very core." In *Zen*, Osho unfolds the paradox of modern life through delightful Zen anecdotes and riddles.

ISBN: 0-312-32049-3   Paperback $11.95/$17.95 Can.

YOUR ANSWERS QUESTIONED

A collection of intriguing, humorous, and surprising inquiries that will encourage you to consider the world in different ways, from different angles, and in new directions. You never know: you might just find some new answers—and some new questions.

ISBN: 0-312-32077-9   Hardcover $18.95/$27.95 Can.

SEX MATTERS

Sex matters to us all. The Osho approach to sex begins with an understanding of the importance of love in our lives, while acknowledging that the journey into love cannot exclude our innate biological energies. The tendency of religions, and society in general, to associate sex with sin is a great misfortune—Osho explains that sex is instead a unique door to self-discovery.

ISBN: 0-312-31630-5   Paperback $14.95/$21.95 Can.

LOVE, FREEDOM, ALONENESS:
THE KOAN OF RELATIONSHIPS

This beautiful new book tackles the whole complexity of issues around relating—from sex to jealousy to compassion, from "falling in a ditch" to "rising in love." Whether you're just beginning a relationship or just ending one, or whether you're part of a happy couple or happy to be uncoupled and alone—reading these pages is like a heart-to-heart with a wise and perceptive friend.

ISBN: 0-312-29162-0   Paperback $14.95/$21.95 Can.

 **OSHO®**   TAKE A NEW LOOK   www.OSHO.cor

 ST. MARTIN'S GRIFFIN